Still, In One Peace

Ronald William Cadmus

Still, In One Peace

Ronald William Cadmus

Winchester, UK
Washington, USA

First published by Circle Books, 2014
Circle Books is an imprint of John Hunt Publishing Ltd., Laurel House, Station Approach,
Alresford, Hants, SO24 9JH, UK
office1@jhpbooks.net
www.johnhuntpublishing.com
www.circle-books.com

For distributor details and how to order please visit the 'Ordering' section on our website.

Text copyright: Ronald William Cadmus 2013

ISBN: 978 1 78279 474 5

A CIP catalogue record for this book is available from the British Library.

Design: Lee Nash

Printed in the USA by Edwards Brothers Malloy

We operate a distinctive and ethical publishing philosophy in all
areas of our business, from our global network of authors to
production and worldwide distribution.

CONTENTS

For my parents
for the places
for the friends
for the parishioners
for the prayers
for the God
for all who have kept me
Still, In One Peace

Foreword

*Upon reading "**Still, In One Peace**",
by Ronald William Cadmus*

Like an honor roll of integrity they come before us, a pantheon of extraordinary people, persons who in spite of their struggles inspire us with their epic examples of bravery and achievements. In a world afflicted with an addiction to mediocrity and plagued by self-interest these paragons of accomplishment speak to us across the ages, urging us to excellence and compelling us to find meaning in spiritual wholeness.

In this gathering of thoughtful observations Ronald Cadmus has assembled a powerful resource for seekers of peace. In each chapter we find a cavalcade of courage, and a testament to powerful living. Far from the examples of selfish conquest that often permeate our contemporary culture these affirmations of excellence call us to an inner power that transcends the ordinary. These are timeless lessons to learn from, enhanced with thoughtful commentary that bring application to our everyday journey of life.

These beautiful examples, ancient and modern, sing to us with eloquent tones. Their voices are life lessons, time-tested songs that awaken in us hopefulness for living. They break our hearts yet mend our wounds. They quiet us and calm us to reflection, yet animate us to action. With each commentary we see the common themes of faith, patience, and peace. In each true-life example we hear an echo of our own challenges and see we are not alone in our quest for inner sanctuary.

"Still, In One Peace" proves itself over and over as an essential source for sacred wellness. It is my hope that as you absorb the powerful truths contained in this book you will be illuminated and inspired. I pray that with each turning of the

page, you will discover a still small voice speaking deep peace to your heart and singing gently to your spirit the wondrous music of grace.

Joseph M. Martin
International Composer, Author, Lecturer

Acknowledgments

For Bill Faulkner, whose faith in me is unwavering. For Astrid Zabriskie, my Administrative Assistant at the Collegiate Church, whose grace, wisdom and creativity encouraged pathways to truth and peace. For Anne Dowling whose passion for peace causes inspired me in the transformation places of solitude. For Jane Killilea and Mary Lou Armiger for reading the text and offering encouragement. For Mom who watched the process with enthusiastic support. For Ms. Baldwin, English Professor at West Virginia Wesleyan and Mrs. Peligrino, English Teacher at Arts High School, who inspired me to see the complimentary colors of words on the other side of the color wheel. For a little church in the Bronx that gave me comfort when I could find no peace. For the Potter's hand that constantly reshapes broken pieces. For the production staff at John Hunt Publishers. For those ecclesiastical centers on city streets, or cathedral forests and the sandy sanctuaries by the ocean, that became the places where I was able to be *Still, in One Peace.*

Introduction

Still, In One Peace

Often we wonder how we survive life, emerging from our situations, still in one piece.

Life is about more than surviving just in one piece. We can go through life in the confident assurance that at the end of the day, after laying to rest the distractions of the day, we can find ourselves *Still, in One Peace*. Regardless of our circumstances, we can be strong, hopeful and secure, discovering we can live each moment, confront every struggle and handle any adversity and find ourselves living *Still, in One Peace*.

The world was focused on Chile and the rescue efforts of thirty-three miners, trapped for over two months in a mine 2300 feet below the surface of the earth, as a bullet-like capsule named Phoenix II brought each miner to the surface. Over a period of thirty-six hours, in an international effort, the miners were rescued, ending their confinement in their dark 90-degree, sweltering tomb. Global media networks covered the miraculous feat. The world cheered their liberation from their hellish nightmare. All 33 men and the team of five rescue workers survived. Each miner had been brought to the surface and reunited with their families. All were in relatively good health. They made it out alive. Still in one piece. As we heard their survival stories, the real miracle became apparent. The lesson of how they were able to stay *Still, in One Peace*.

They emerged in one piece, in good spirits, with sincere gratitude to be alive. We heard of the horrifying uncertainty of their first seventeen days, when no one knew if they were alive, or the miners wondering if efforts were being made to rescue them. They endured in absolute obscurity, rationing food, conserving drinking water, water contained in barrels tainted with oil. They encouraged each other to survive. The stories of optimism, hope and spiritual stamina, gave us insight into their ability to stay *Still, in One Peace.* A peace that kept them from surrendering to their entombment, as they remained hopeful against the prospect of their own deaths.

Several days after their rescue the world learned of another disaster in the tragic fatality of miners in China. We try to make sense out of the miraculous outcome of one disaster and the disastrous conclusion of another, reminding us that life is unreasonable as it deals its harsh blows. As life is fired at us point blank, we go through experiences, wondering how we survived them. How we came through them still in one piece.

We've been discouraged by economic depression, frightened by terrorist threats, disheartened by loss of jobs, left destitute through home foreclosures, torn apart by racial tensions and hate crimes, made insecure by threats of nuclear proliferation, demoralized by the decline of our ethics, defeated by natural disasters that leave people in poverty, homeless, diseased and hopeless. The world still suffers from the ravaging effects of war. This is not to mention the onslaught of daily assaults on our minds and spirits from our incessant problems encountered each day. We have known the tragedy of national disasters with the Hurricanes Katrina and Sandy, and most recently Typhoon Haiyan in the Philippines. We have seen the suffering and horror of the massacre of 20 children, six and seven years old, and their teachers in Sandy Hook Elementary School in Newtown, Connecticut and the mass shootings in a movie theater in Aurora, Colorado leaving our nation, world and families shattered in pieces. The George Zimmerman and Trayvon Martin murder trial in Florida has left our nation polarized, if not in pieces. The Mid East crisis in Syria is another reminder of our fragile, global peace. We're amazed if we can survive it all and emerge from each situation, still in one piece.

Circumstances can crush us, but they do not have to defeat us. Cancer might metastasize to every cell in our bodies. It cannot terminate our spirit. Nor touch our spirit. We can resolve to seek that place of peace within. When we do, we will find ourselves *Still, in One Peace.*

For this peace to be real, it must be unaffected by outside and inside circumstances. Despite those circumstances, we make a choice to be still, in that One place of peace. We should not internalize outside influences, nor should we be governed by internal conditions. We can battle cancer, yet live our most vital moments in positive ways. Love with our greatest yearnings, even if the end of the road is clearly defined and bleak. We can hope in promises yet to be born. Live to the fullest of our ability. Dream, though surrounded by discouragements. Sing, when bound by darkness. When we cannot remember anymore, in the case of millions dealing with Alzheimer's, to know there is a Spirit, the One, who will always remember us. If peace is to be real, we cannot allow it to be negated by internal and external circumstances. We must turn to find that peace within. And find that when we do, we can be *Still, in One Peace.*

We don't have to go through life, surviving it merely in one piece. We can go through it, living in the confident reassurance that we can be *Still, in One Peace.*

I want to acknowledge my friend Dr. Len Sweet, author and theologian, who signs his letters to me with a blessed reassurance, *"Still, In One Peace."* For his permission to let me use that phrase as the inspiration and title for this book, I thank him for the peace his friendship and writings have provided, and for the opportunity he gave me to encourage you to know that you can live each day of your life, *Still, in One Peace.*

RWC

Chapter One

Ludwig van Beethoven

You never enjoy the world aright, till the sea itself floweth in your veins, till you are clothed with the heavens, and crowned with the stars, and perceive yourself to be the sole heir of the whole world, and more than so because men are in it who are every one sole heirs as well as you.
Thomas Tracherne

If water derives lucidity from stillness, how much more the faculties of the mind! The mind of the sage, being in repose, becomes the mirror of the universe, the speculum of all creation.
Chuang Tzu

Actor Gary Oldman starred as Ludwig van Beethoven in Columbia Picture's **Immortal Beloved,** a movie about searching for the identity of Beethoven's unnamed *Immortal Beloved.* mentioned in a perplexing letter discovered after his death. The search for her identity reveals Beethoven's bleak past, deepest passions and the creative genius of his music, composed throughout much of his debilitating hearing and eventual deafness.

"Several reasons are attributed to his deafness, among them the violent digestive disorders that plagued him, frightful attacks of typhus, to his having become drenched while composing music outdoors during tumultuous rains. Other possibilities were the exposure to a draft on a hot summer's day; to rheumatism, as well as a congenital weakness in his auditory canal."

It has been suggested that the onset of his hearing impairment resulted from brutal beatings by his father. Historians claim the ruthless severity of his father caused them to believe "that there were few days when he was not beaten in order to compel him to sit at the piano." His father was angry with Beethoven's enjoyment of improvisation at the keyboard, to which his father said, "Are you fooling around? Go away or I'll box your ears."

A boyhood friend wrote, "There were few days when he was not flogged or locked up in the cellar. He was deprived of sleep, awakened by his father at midnight to practice piano."

One wonders how he survived such treatment and how he was able to find himself still in one piece when he woke up each morning, having endured those merciless abuses.

Beethoven admitted, "When I am playing or composing my affliction hampers me least." He was referring to the affliction of his hearing but I suspect the suffering inflicted upon him by his father contributed to his finding solace and escape in music.

Musical historians said, "The onset of his deafness was the painful chrysalis within which his 'heroic' style as a composer came to maturity." Pain shaped Beethoven. It shapes us as well.

In the movie there is a horrific scene of a teenage Beethoven in which we observe the external forces of fear forced upon him in his harsh world. He escapes his father's fists, climbs out the bedroom window, shimmies down the roof and runs frantically through the forest. His desperate retreat is underscored musically by the creative genius of Beethoven's 9th Symphony, "Ode to Joy." Free from the horrors of this cruel childhood moment, free to be "like a dreamer, to combine and re-combine the stuff of reality, in accordance with his desires, into previously undreamed of forms and structures."

Beethoven emerges from the forest, coming to a placid lake in the middle of the night. Stepping into the water he wades a short distance from the shore, placing his shattered life into the "chrysalis" embryonic security of the water, slowly immersing himself in the taciturn world and sanctuary of the water. As he reposes there, the triumphant music of the closing phrases of Ode to Joy carries him to celestial glory.

As the camera lifts high above Beethoven's submerged body, the lake becomes ablaze with the mirrored reflection of a host of stars. Escaping his trauma, he becomes lost in wonder, love and praise. One with the stars. The water flowed in his veins. He had become clothed with the heavens, crowned with the stars. He becomes sole heir of the whole world, in his world of isolation, beneath the water, in an eternal silence with the divine celestial illuminations flowing through him. His life was united with the stars, creating one of cinematography's most splendid and breathtaking scenes. There was no distinguishing aspect of Beethoven's body, the stars and his music. He was absorbed in celestial brilliance.

Beethoven wrote, "Only in my divine art do I find the support which enables me to sacrifice the best part of my life to the heavenly Muses." The words of the writer he admired, Herder, encouraged him. Herder said, "Risk everything, then! What God has granted to you, nobody can rob you of. Indeed, he granted it to you, to you, brave man."

Another admired writer, Zacharius Werner enjoined him to seek, "The great good of self-completion in creating – you are the mirror image of the Eternal."

This is what Bruce Davey, producer of **Immortal Beloved** captured in this scene. In his writing *Tagebuch*, Beethoven extracts from Sir William Jones' "Hymn to Narayenae" to raise the poet's soul to heights of ecstasy:

Oh! Guide my fancy sight,
Oh! Raise from cumbrous ground
My soul in rapture drown'd
That fearless it may soar on wings of fire.

Through his deafness, he found life and integrated himself into the transcendence of the infinite stars. For Beethoven, celestial imagery becomes a prime metaphor of the "sense of identity with a larger power of creative energy."

In Maynard Solomon's book **Late Beethoven**, Solomon says, "Beethoven's urge to retreat to conflict-free surroundings frequently has religious overtones." Beethoven wrote as a heading to the *Allegretto vivace* of the Dona Nobis Pacem of **Missa Solemnis Op 123**, "Plea for inner and outer peace." "Calm, joy, the infinite and nature are threaded like beads on an unbroken strand of associated ideas. Tranquility and freedom are the greatest treasures." In these qualities, Beethoven found his peace.

This scene in **Immortal Beloved** is worth remembering. Beethoven immersed himself in the stillness of the living streams of the waters of life and found his soul and music, his creative genius, nurtured by being *Still, in One Peace.* United with the stars. With heaven. With God. Here he found his tranquility and freedom.

We are all heirs not only of his music and genius, but heirs of the world if we find ourselves, *Still, in One Peace.*

Beethoven's biographer concludes, "In clusters of images centering upon the starry skies, the mysteries of space, the turning of the heavenly spheres, the attributes of the deity against the backdrop of the celestial vault, the immensity of the night, Beethoven seems to have found a natural outlet for his feelings of awe and wonder."

We can too, if we image-center ourselves in the Still place, in that One peace. There we find our wholeness. There we will hear the music of life. Our own Ode to joy! Until we do, we will never enjoy the world aright! The mind of the sage, the mind of Beethoven, or our own minds, when that mind is in repose, becomes the mirror of the universe, the speculum of all creation. We become one with the stars. We become still, in their peace.

Beethoven, having suffered the harsh abuse of his father, found hope in the words of Shiller's text for the libretto of his 9th Symphony. In the stillness of the One who offers peace, Beethoven immortalized Shiller's words:

Brothers beyond the starry firmament
there surely dwells a loving Father.

In those stars, in the stillness of their light, he finally found his One true peace. The divine love within his soul. In his music he found that love that escaped him with his earthly father.

In a work by Christopher Christian Sturm, **Reflections on the Works of God in Nature**, Beethoven had underlined:

King of heaven! Sovereign Ruler of worlds! Father of angels and men! O that my ideas were as vast and sublime as the extent of the heavens, that I might worthily contemplate thy magnificence! O that I could raise them to those innumerable worlds, where thou dost manifest thy glory ever more than on our globe; that as I walk it present from flower to flower, I might then go from star to star, till I come to the august sanctuary where thou sittest upon the throne of thy glory! But my wishes are useless, as long as I am but a traveler on this globe, I cannot fully know the beauty and magnitude of those celestial worlds, till my soul be freed from this gross body. In expectation of this, as long as I shall live, I will lift up my voice and invite men to celebrate the glory of the Lord.

If you have days when you wonder, with all you have been through, how you're still in one piece, you will never enjoy the world aright, until you place yourself in that still, One peace. Be still. Repose. Quiet the mind.

Listen to Beethoven's music. Let it flow in your veins. Let it clothe you with the heavens and crown you with stars and perceive yourself to be the sole heir of the whole world. Find that still, peaceful place for your own life. Be in One peace. It's a pretty wise thing to do from time to time. All the time. Go from flower to flower. From star to star. From piece to peace. Until you come to that august sanctuary where you can be *Still, in One Peace.*

Resource: *Late Beethoven, Music, Thought, Imagination,* Maynard Solomon, University of California Press, October 4, 2004

Chapter Two

Helen Keller

Once I knew only darkness and stillness... my life was without past or future... but a little word from the fingers of another fell into my hand that clutched at emptiness, and my heart leaped to the rapture of living.
Helen Keller

In truth, to attain to interior peace, one must be willing to pass through the contrary to peace. Such is the teaching of the sages.
Swami Brahmananda

It wasn't a question of willingness on Helen Keller's part, in her desire to find inner tranquility, that she should be "willing to pass through the contrary to peace" in order to attain profound, intimate peace.

An illness in infancy left her blind and deaf. She had no choice. Her world of darkness and stillness left her without a "past or future," as well as a fear of living in the "now." Life seems unreasonable as it deals its harsh blows.

Living in darkness and stillness, her hands clutched only at emptiness, until her teacher, Ann Sullivan entered her life, leaving an imprint upon her hand and soul. Together, they began the journey that would pass through the excruciating, contrary aspects of serenity, bringing Helen's life to light and voice.

For Helen, "stillness" was a nightmare. She said she had no "reality." No past. No future. Stillness represented "inertness," not tranquility or peacefulness. In her black void, she felt a stabbing "emptiness." She was a self-confined vessel, an abyss of obscurity, with a mind that heard no sound, and a body devoid of light. "A little girl without a dialect."

Yet she could feel warm sun against her body, smell flowers in her desperation to know beauty, feel gentle breezes against her flesh, and joy in raindrops and snowflakes caressing her eyelashes. As a child, she loved climbing trees and smelling blossoms.

One day, a finger altered her life. A little word from a finger that fell into her hand, penetrating her world. That one touch caused her heart to leap to the rapture of living.

To attain interior peace, she traveled the pathway "contrary to peace." It led to the soaring rapture of her heart. One imprint on a hand reaching for emptiness, allowed Helen to leap into the stillness, of One peace. In that peace she found hope despite her deprivation. The imprint of a touch is life-changing!

That truth allowed Helen Keller to say, "Once I knew *only* darkness and stillness." Once she knew... her previous state of being. But the moment a finger touched the palm of her hand her world was illuminated. *Once I knew, once I felt that touch...* my heart leaped to the rapture of living. This moment of acknowledgement changed her life, bringing it out of darkness, inertness and emptiness, opening a world of hope, peace and light.

Helen Keller said, "The mystery of language was revealed to me. I knew then that W A T E R meant that wonderful cool something that was flowing over my hand. That living word awakened my soul, gave it light, joy and set it free."

Ann touched her not only with the imprint of her fingers but the imprint and gift of her love, reminding us that everything we do must be done out of love.

In telling her childhood story, specifically the one in which her teacher first arrived at her home, Helen shares how she had been inwardly crying for some sensation of light:

Have you ever been at sea in a dense fog, when it seemed as if a tangible white darkness shut you in, and the great ship, tense and anxious, groped her way toward the shore with plummet and sounding-line and you waited with beating heart for something to happen? I was like that ship before my education began, only I was without compass or sounding-line and had no way of knowing how near the harbor was. Light! Give me light! was the wordless cry of my soul and the light of love shone in me that very hour. I felt approaching footsteps. I stretched out my hand as I supposed it to be my mother. Someone took it and I was caught up and held close in the arms of her who had come to reveal all things to me and more then all things else, to love me.

Until that epiphany, until "once she knew" the devotion and love of Ann Sullivan, her life was "in the still dark world in which I lived, where there was no strong sentiment or tenderness."

Once that finger fell into that hand that had been clutching at emptiness, once she began learning about life, love and beauty through words, she finally arrived at an emotionally still place of peace. Remembering that day she said,

It would have been difficult to find a happier child than I was as I lay in my crib at the close of that eventful day. I lived over and over the joy it had brought me, and for the first time longed for a new day to come.

Long before I learned to do a sum in arithmetic or describe the shape of the earth, Miss Sullivan had taught me to find beauty in the fragrant woods, in every blade of grass and in the curves and dimples of my baby sister's hand. She linked my earliest thoughts with nature and made me feel that "birds and flowers and I were happy peers.

In harmony with beauty and life! This indeed is a place where we find ourselves to be **Still, in One Peace.**

A little word from the fingers of another that fell into her hand opened her to a world of beauty and peace. It opened her to the beauty of her soul, in which she was able to find her lasting "stillness in peace."

Helen Keller concluded her autobiography with an illuminating thought. "Thus it is that my friends have made the story of my life in a thousand ways, they have turned my limitations into beautiful privilege and enabled me to walk serene and happy in the shadow cast by my deprivation."

Serene and happy, a soul that is *Still, in One Peace*. Composed. Happy. Yet living in the shadow cast by her deprivation. An acknowledgement that despite her darkness and her silence, her deprivation of being blind and deaf, it is love that touches us to wholeness. A little word, from the finger of another spelling "doll" and "water", a loving touch from another in the deprivation of our lives, can make our hearts leap for joy. That loving touch helps us survive, if not overcome our deprivations.

Whose finger has touched your life, with little words of encouragement and love, hope and joy?

What little word of love, hope and life have you written with your finger on another's hand? What little word of encouragement and compassion have you allowed to fall into a heart that is clutching at emptiness?

Your one word, your single touch, can be the moment someone finds themselves *Still, in One Peace*, though they are surrounded by the shadows of their deprivations. Your touch can awaken their soul, give it light, joy and even set it free! Despite those deprivations, a touch will help us find the place where we can be *Still, in One Peace*.

Resource: *The Autobiography of Helen Keller, The Story of My Life*, Helen Keller and Ann Sullivan 1903 NY, NY Doubleday

Chapter Three

Maria von Trapp

Blessed are the single-hearted, for they shall enjoy much peace. If you refuse to be hurried and pressed, if you stay your soul on God, nothing can keep you from that clearness of spirit which is life and peace. In that stillness you will know what His will is.

Amy Carmichael

Never be in a hurry; do everything quietly and in a calm spirit. Do not lose your inner peace for anything whatsoever, even if your whole world seems upset.

St. Francis de Sales

It was a thrilling experience to share a day with Maria von Trapp, when I invited her to deliver the keynote message at The Founder's Day Celebrations at the Ocean Grove Auditorium, in Ocean Grove, New Jersey, where I was program director for special events. On the wall of my office is a treasured picture of my six-year-old daughter Laurie with Baroness von Trapp. The picture was featured in a State newspaper celebrating the event attended by 5000 admirers of this Austrian heroine immortalized in the Academy Award winning film, **The Sound of Music**, starring Julie Andrews.

At dinner we shared a delightful conversation about the film and its depiction of her life as a nun, who became the governess of Captain von Trapp's children, eventually marrying the Baron. Maria told me that the film accurately depicted her life, except for one scene. "We didn't flee the Nazi officers by singing as we walked across the Austrian Alps." "That would have been unwise," she said, "in our attempt to secretly escape." This was a delightful, charming moment with Maria.

Recently revisiting the movie, I recalled the treasured memory of spending time with Maria von Trapp. Near the end of the movie, Maria, the Captain and children flee the concert hall after winning first prize in the Salzburg Music Festival, as German authorities wait to escort Baron von Trapp to his military assignment in the Third Reich. They seek refuge in the convent where Maria previously spent time preparing to become a nun prior to meeting the handsome Baron who changed the course of her life. The Reverend Mother provided asylum among the cemetery tombs. There is chaos among the sisters of the convent, as they conspire to hide the von Trapp family before the Nazis arrive.

Hearing the blaring sirens of the approaching Nazis' automobiles, the nuns frantically run through the corridors of the convent. Observing their frenzy, the Reverend Mother motioning for them to adapt to their reserved protocol, says, "Slowly, Slowly," to which they resume their decorum. They begin walking respectively, prayerfully, arriving at the gate, nodding solemnly to the soldiers who burst their way through the entrance of the cobbled stone courtyard.

I've used this illustration in seminars when speaking about handling job performance, stress, and anxiety. "Never be in a hurry; do everything quietly and in a calm spirit. Do not lose your inner peace for anything whatsoever, even if your whole world seems upset." I remind myself of this constantly when I overreact to distressing circumstances. I try not to fly off the handle, giving the impression that I can't manage my frustrations or anger, or the situation.

This is helpful in keeping our lives centered, *Still, in One Peace*. Otherwise, if you don't, when life is disturbing, and you lose your grounding of inner peace, or your "single-heartedness," chances are you'll find after the disconcerting incident that you are *just* still in one piece. You've survived your circumstances but the residual anxiety and nervous tension incessantly vibrate like a tuning fork. You're not really in a calm place, though you have survived in one piece. You can say that you survived in one piece, but it could be one, big piece or bag of nerves. Just feel your heart racing. Take your pulse and blood pressure. Or just look at how many times you continue to recount the unpleasant experience or how many times you need to take a sedative.

Do not lose your inner peace for anything whatsoever. Stay *Still, in One Peace.*

As the von Trapp family flees the safety of the monastic walls, the nuns listen to the futile attempts of the drivers to start the sputtering engines of their automobiles. Peering at their frustration one nun says, "Reverend Mother, we have sinned!" "What is it, my child?" the Reverend Mother inquires, at which moment two nuns, calmly and reverently bring from beneath their habits, oily hands holding two distributors from the cars' engines.

This humorous anecdote teaches a wise lesson of doing everything by remaining quiet and in a calm way. Staying single-hearted in peace. There is a look of gentle understanding and appreciation on the face of the Reverend Mother who breathes a sigh of relief for their quick thinking. The look is also one of absolution, for their not so sinful conspiracy.

These nuns had maintained an undeterred, quiet, calm spirit. They were reminded not to be harried or pressed but to stay their souls on God. In that stillness, in the clarity of the Spirit, they were part of a greater plan, if you will, God's plan to aid the von Trapp family, guiding them to their escape over the mountains on their journey to freedom so that they could find their dreams. As Rodgers and Hammerstein's lyrics said, "A dream that will need all the love you can give, everyday of your life, for as long as you live."

All the love, all the calmness of spirit, or the tranquility of thought, all the determination to live undeterred by the pressing issues of life: stayed, steady, strong, and *Still, in One Peace*, not just in a momentary experience, but as a way of living, all of your life, "for as long as you live."

I thought of these wise implications as I sat in a wonderful conversation with Maria von Trapp. Being with her I found myself *Still, in One Peace*. The peacefulness of her presence. That peace was in her face, now as an elderly woman living at the Trapp Family Lodge in Stowe, Vermont.

All of her life she stayed her soul on God and nothing could keep her from that clearness of spirit which is life and peace. When my life becomes agitated, frenzied, anxious and pressing, I hear God say to me, "Slowly, slowly," and I take a sudden pause, and slip back into the decorum of peacefulness and stillness, the place where I gain a clearer sense of His purpose and will for my life in every circumstance. I find myself, *Still, in One Peace*. That stillness, that peace, helps me get over a lot of mountains.

When I heard that Maria von Trapp died, I said a quiet prayer for her. I look at her picture with my daughter, tender, affectionate imagining just how Maria must have been when her children were young during those governess years in Austria. Imagining her in the embraceable love of God, I thought this is just how she and God were looking into each other's single-hearted gaze, and He saw in her face, His precious child, that at last she was *Still, in One Peace*.

Chapter Four

Olympic Games 2010

It is good to realize that if love and peace can prevail on earth, and if we can teach our children to honor nature's gifts, the joys and beauties of the outdoors will be here forever.
President Jimmy Carter

Is it any wonder that the viewing audience for the opening ceremonies of the 2010 23rd Olympic Games in Vancouver, British Columbia, was the largest ever to watch the televised global spectacle inaugurating the 16 days of international competition?

We have been discouraged by worldwide, economic depression, frightened by terrorist threats against the human race, disheartened by unemployment, left abandoned through home foreclosures, torn apart by racial tensions, made insecure by threats of nuclear proliferation, demoralized by the decline of ethical values, defeated by natural disasters in New Orleans, Asia and Haiti, Hurricane Sandy, floods in Colorado, wild fires in the mid west. All allowing us to see the pain inflicted on our lives, the face of poverty, homelessness, disease and hopelessness. And each day we see the ravages of war. This is not to mention the barrage of daily assaults on our psyches and spirits from our incessant personal problems encountered each day.

Watching the Olympics is like discovering a breathing place for our souls. We inhale the fresh, pure air of the pristine, snow-covered terrain of Canada, captured in High Definition wide-screen images in our homes; we get in touch with the human spirit; with the magnificence of our planet; with the optimism and fortitude of each athlete. We find ourselves poised on the ice with champions who show us the shape and form of human gracefulness.

The Olympic Games help us realize that if love, peace, sportsmanship and fair play can prevail on earth, through its youth, then there is something of hope that endures. That can change the world. Shape it into one human family of love, as the children of earth run swifter, higher, stronger, to achieve their ideals and live their dreams. To capture, in the words sung poignantly by Sarah McLaughlin at the opening ceremonies, those "ordinary miracle days." We see their sweet dreams of imagined possibilities.

This is all achieved at a cost as we aim for success, break speed records, and raise the bar with new degrees of difficulty in each competition in an attempt to clutch the gold.

Sacrifice and failure precedes triumph. We do not mount a platform to receive a medal without realizing the pain and loss, the defeat, failure and mistakes that occur in pursuit of our aspirations, tragically witnessed in the heartbreaking fatality of the young Republic of Georgia luger Nodar Kumaritashvili at Whistle Mountain.

Perhaps, as anguishing as that moment was, his death occurring only a few hours before the world converged into the arena for the opening exercises, the sobering comprehension of his shattered dream and life, replayed through the video of his face beneath the plastic guard of his helmet, became etched in the memory of determination and hope, as he prepared to race down the luge. Looking into his eyes we gained the glimpse of what the purpose of life was for him – *it was to have a purpose in life.*

To let "purpose prevail," less concerned for the risks inherent in that purpose, in each athlete's pursuit of that joy, purpose and dream.

When we fail and fall, we pick ourselves up and simply try again. The Olympic torch inspiring us to make our dreams burn brightly, inspiring humanity to be brave, strong, true.

In a Life magazine ad sponsored by Philip 66 Gas Company honoring the 1984 Olympic Athletes, one of our divers in the

Summer Olympics was pictured executing his precision dive. Accompanying the ad was this statement:

Everyone starts at the bottom. Real winning
comes in not staying there in United States diving;
real winning comes when young people learn that it is okay to be
    afraid, that there is no shame in failing;
and as they learn to dazzle the air and knife the water they learn
something much more important, that the most
soaring triumphs are in
simply trying again.

We marvel at an Olympian's agility and speed separated by seconds at the finish line after excruciating cross-country heats, precision figure skating, challenging mogul hills, or downhill runs. In a flash, something goes amiss, bringing the force of speed and physics together. Skaters spin out, two Korean skaters fall and slide to defeat, opening the way for Apollo Ono to win a medal. Skiers tumble off course. Scores shift a hopeful competitor off the chairs of medal contention. Dreams are shattered. The medal becomes elusive. In the case of the Georgian luger, life is lost, traumatizing teammates, shocking the world. We marvel at the human spirit, its soaring triumph, in simply trying again. The competition goes on, with a deeper sense of pride because of the passions in the life of one athlete whose death reminded them of the dreams he pursued.

Sixty Thousand people in a stadium and millions watching around the world, found themselves standing, still, in a moment of silence, in one common bond of humanity embraced by love and peace in memory of a fallen athlete. Still, in One, in the One Spirit, of Peace.

One life brought a stadium to its feet in silence and stillness. Immobile. Heads bowed, as if to remind us that our power, grace, strength and fortitude, does not come from us, or from the success of our own achievements, but flows into and through us as gift. We, the children of the earth are the vessels for the gifts of the earth. Still, in One peaceful reflection. Did you not have a tear within your eye in that sacramental moment of stillness? The heart of humanity was beating as one. Standing in the solidarity of peace. In quietness. His death did not mar the beginning of the 23rd Olympic Games. It colored the design and purpose of the days to follow – to pursue, not gold, but to pursue joy and peace, honoring the nature of our human spirit and fortitude. Acknowledging we are not merely superheroes, fearless athletes, but children of the earth imbued with all its promises and possibilities, claiming all that life has to give. To give all the love that is within us to share.

There is hope beyond defeat. We soar, facing the challenge to fill our world, life, ourselves with love and peace our whole lives through. Through these Olympians, we realize that somewhere in this uncertain world, children have learned to pursue lives of purpose as well as competition, of sport as well as character. They inspire generations.

They honor nature's gift as well as the gift of their own natures; their own souls, their own hearts. Honoring the love, peace, joy and purpose that we bring to life, as we live *Still, in One Peace*. In the peace and joy of simply being alive, filled with ambition and dreams. With a desire to make life meaningful. The world better. Safe. Peaceful. Spirit imbued.

The singer, Barbra Streisand, made an inspiring statement at her New Year's Eve Concert that ushered in the new Millennium 2000.

In this first hour, of the first morning, of the first day, of a new year,
a new decade, a new century, a new millennium.
we all want to change the world into a better place
but that's an overwhelming task
I think all we can only change is ourselves, a little bit at a time
because that's the only thing we have control over

as we change ourselves inside,
I believe we can change the world.

The backdrop of the Olympic competitions is the grandeur, majesty and beauty of nature, in the splendid snow-covered mountain ranges and forests in Canada. I'm swept up in the breathtaking images of towering mountain peaks, as on the landscape is seen a climber who has conquered the harsh cliffs and ice-covered mountains, reaching the summit, looking out into the purity of nature's canvas, as John Williams' theme to the Olympians blares with its trumpet fanfare. That athlete stands nobly on the summit in a portrait of harmony with the elements, the earth, the air, the space, the dreams and the visions as the world opens its arms to hold his heart. He's at the top of his game. We feel like we are standing there with him. He represents what humanity can be, as humanity stands *Still, in One Peace* within the world. At the top of his world, we feel his dream to change the world into a better place. We change it by changing ourselves inside – by living the dream, setting our goals high, believing in ourselves, believing in humankind.

"It is good to realize that if love and peace can prevail on earth, and if we can teach our children to honor nature's gifts, the joys and beauties of the outdoors will be here forever."

If we can teach our children to honor the gifts of their own nature, if they reach more for stars than gold, for dreams then recognition, to teach them to respect the landscape on which they compete, to love one another, the earth upon which they discipline their bodies and strengthen their determination, forge their character, then the earth will birth within them the gifts of the spirit of the earth that calls them to be children of the earth. Honoring the gift of the earth, the gift of life, that gives them their moments in which to aspire and achieve.

Doing this, the joys and beauties of the outdoors will be here forever, and those outdoors, all of nature, will be infused within the spirit, love and peace of humankind.

The Aborigine Indian tribes were featured in the opening ceremonies of the Olympic Games. Those Indians teach us much of the Spirit of the Earth, in which we find our stillness and peace. It was Chief Seattle who said,

The great American Indian nations taught us to live as if the next seven generations mattered. We do not inherit the earth from our grandparents; we are borrowing it from our grandchildren. We owe it to our children and our children's children to leave the land in much better shape than it is today. You must teach your children that the ground beneath their feet is the ashes of our grandfathers. So that they respect the land, tell your children that the earth is rich with the lives of our kin. Teach your children what we have taught our children; that the earth is our mother. Whatever befalls the earth befalls the sons of the earth. Man did not weave the web of life; he is merely a strand in it. Whatever he does to the web, he does to himself.

When I watch the Olympics, the faces of our youth, there is a belief that flows within me that the joys and beauties of the world will be here forever. That the joys and beauties of the children of earth will be here forever. If love and peace prevails through them. If we stay *Still, in One Peace*. "It is good to realize" this, as we look to the youth of our world for hope. We cheer them on as they dream to change the world. As they love and protect the best that earth has to offer. As they dream to be the world's truest gifts. We will remember always the face of a young Georgian athlete, frozen in the eyes of our souls, reminding us to go for the... dream! The joy and beauty of his life and his fellow champions will be here forever. They remind us of our wonderful world and the real prize of peace that lies at the heart of the human spirit.

Chapter Five

Unaffected by Outside Circumstances

Each one has to find his peace from within. And peace to be real must be unaffected by outside circumstances.
Mahatma Gandhi

Outside circumstances can break us. However, inside conditions, like terminal illness, depression, debilitating maladies, chronic problems, emotional fatigue and fear cause internal fissures as well.

How do we unearth that inner peace, when both external *and* internal circumstances assault us like mudslides in the aftermath of a deluge of misfortune, eroding our fortitude, often leading to desperate measures and tragic ends? Our minds and bodies are tossed like splintered houses into swollen riverbanks of despair. We get swallowed up by circumstances. We become fatigued fighting the emotional currents. They leave high water marks, the circumstantial tides which leave us covered with mold and silt, virtually destroying every treasured aspect of our lives. Just thirteen miles from my home lies the destruction and debris of Hurricane Sandy, leaving lives ravaged and people homeless. Though thousands are left in despair they are struggling to begin their lives again. In their determination we understand – we can find real peace, if we look within, and not at our circumstances.

The King of Pop, Michael Jackson is an example of how outside and inside circumstances can destroy us. His desperation manifested in an anesthetized coma, to deal with sleep deprivation, while his body swirled around, exacerbated by demonizing, nightmarish circumstances, rendered him incapable of handling those circumstances. Though saddened by his untimely death, we should be dismayed that the circumstances of his life drove him to recline at night, injected with a solution to place him in a comatose state, suspended in an emulsion of circumstances. Inner peace eluded him. Rather than seeking the peace to be found within, he shut himself down, shut himself off from it, only to be awakened by turning off the intravenous needle, still finding himself in his world that held no true sense of deep peace.

What happens when you cannot turn to your own body to find the comfort and solace you desperately seek? Mahatma Gandhi's words are poignant: "We must find our peace *from* within." We do not bring it within. We *find* it within. We are Spiritual at the core of our lives. This core is something we call our "soul." Too often we find false comfort zones, outside of ourselves. There is a peace, a still, sure and certain peace that is real, unaffected by circumstances. It is a peace that in order for it to be found, to be real, must be sought after. Within.

Circumstances can crush us, yes. But they do not have to defeat us. Cancer might metastasize to every crevice of our bodies. It cannot terminate our Spirit. Nor even touch our Spirit. We can resolve to seek that place of peace within – to be *Still, in One Peace.* For this peace to be real, it must be unaffected by outside and inside circumstances. Despite those circumstances, we make a choice to be Still, in that One place of peace. We should not internalize outside influences, nor should we be governed by internal circumstances. We can battle cancer, yet live our most vital moments in positive ways. Love with our greatest yearnings, even if the end of the road is clearly defined and appears bleak. Hope in promises yet to be born. Live to the fullest of our ability. Dream, though surrounded by discouragements. Sing, when bound by darkness, trusting in the nature of the nightingale. When we cannot remember anymore, in the case of millions dealing with Alzheimer's to know there is a Spirit, the One, who will always remember us. If peace is to be real, we cannot allow it to be negated by internal and external circumstances. We must turn to find that peace *within*.

In my devotional time, I use the Book of Common Prayer in addressing my personal needs. The book also reminds me to pray for others. I think of one particular person for whom I pray, especially in the climate of political, partisan bickering that daily assaults us with attacks on those in authority. We are bombarded by opinions hell bent on destroying the character and Spirit of another. The prayer, to which I refer, is for our leaders, particularly the President of the United States. Let me refer to that prayer to make my point:

> *Most heartily we beseech thee, with thy favor to behold*
> *(The President and the Congress of the United States, and others in*
>   *authority),*
> *and so replenish them with thy grace that they may always incline*
>   *to thy will*
> *and walk in thy way. Prosper all good counsels and all just works,*
>   *that*
> *peace and happiness, truth and righteousness, religion and piety,*
> *may be established among us throughout all generations.*

It is not an issue that I prayed for Bush or today, pray for Obama. The issue is that I pray for the President – with no partisan inclinations that God favors a particular party. Mine. When I hear slanderous comments about a particular President, mentioned by name, or articulated through offensive caricature, it is apparent we have forfeited the right Spirit within, negating our civility and grace by mean-spiritedness.

It is humbling to pray for those in authority. Humbling to mention the President by name. Humbling to attend a prayer breakfast with the President of the United States, seeing the President's head bowed in prayer. It is even more humbling to be in a private room with the President of the United States with just a few people in prayer. It is extremely humbling joining hands in a circle of leaders turning for guidance and strength. It is profoundly humbling to hold the hand of the President of the United States in prayer. Just the two of you, in the same room. Sharing one prayer. I have had such a humbling experience, as together we stood *Still, in One Peace*. I have been in the same room with different Presidents. But this one moment of prayer, with one particular head of state, reminded me of this Book of Common Prayer's petition that I "heartily continue to pray for those in authority." That moment was with Richard M. Nixon.

In July 1989 my Uncle, Karl Klein, died after a long battle with a malignant brain tumor. Since I was a colleague of Norman Vincent Peale at the Collegiate Church in New York City, my uncle had access to Dr. Peale on several occasions, the most meaningful moments being during his illness, when he had opportunities to be in Peale's presence or to receive encouraging phone calls from him. Karl also admired President Richard Nixon, always wishing he could meet him. Though I had been in correspondence with President Nixon on numerous occasions prior to becoming a minister with the Collegiate Church in 1981, it was not until my installation as one of the ministers of America's historic congregation, that I had the opportunity to meet the Nixon family. The Nixons and the Peales were dear friends. Julie Nixon Eisenhower helped facilitate my Uncle's dreams to meet her father. Though one scheduled appointment was cancelled because of Karl's deteriorating health, we finally arranged the date of May 17, 1989 for that meeting in Nixon's Upper Saddle River New Jersey office where he resided with his wife Pat Nixon.

Though Karl would have coveted engaging in stimulating political banter or issues about world concerns, the conversation took a different path, in the "heart to heart" talk he had with Nixon. The conversation lasted more than an hour, as my Aunt and two cousins watched their father and husband comforted by Richard Nixon's supportive hand that never left my uncle's arm as they sat side by side.

Knowing Karl had been a Thunderbolt pilot during World War II, Nixon shared a few war stories, with a particular thought he wanted to drive into my uncle's heart. Nixon asked him, "Karl, what was one of the first things you learned in your training to be a Thunderbolt pilot?" Comprehending the question, but unable to articulate his thoughts through his altered speech, Nixon resolutely grabbed his arm and said with vigor, "The first thing you were taught, Karl, was to keep your eyes on the horizon!" "Always keep your eyes on the horizon!" "Are you going to let this cancer defeat you?! Karl, just keep your eyes on the horizon!"

I wondered, in looking at the two of them, who gave Nixon those simple, yet encouraging words of advice when he resigned the office of the Presidency following the crimes of Watergate. Both men, sitting before me had a cancer, a death looming over them. Before our meeting concluded, Nixon asked me to pray. I held his hand, and with my other hand held my Uncle's hand. Two men. One the mighty President of the United States. The other, my wonderful Uncle, whose life was swiftly slipping away through cancer.

The realization then hit me. It was not a mighty President holding the hand of my broken uncle. I was holding the hand of two broken people. Both encouraging each other, through their own personal experience and brokenness, to look to the horizon that will always bring one's life to be *Still, in One Peace*. As we held our hands, I knew that we were all broken people in need of the profound goodness and grace of God, the One who holds us *Still, in One Peace*.

When I finished praying, Richard Nixon placed his hand on my shoulder and said, "That was eloquent!" Grace, when shared with the hearts of others, is always eloquent in the love and mercy, kindness and goodness that it shares, no matter how well crafted in thought, or how simply shared through heartfelt and soul-filled expression. We all stood together in the fellowship of one human being caring for another, in that profound Still place, where peace is found. Real peace.

Several months later Karl died. Four years later Norman Peale died. At Peale's service in Marble Collegiate Church on Fifth Avenue in New York City, I sat next to Nixon and his daughter Tricia Nixon Cox. A few months later, Richard Nixon died and was buried at his library in California, next to his dear wife Pat.

I remembered Nixon's words when he spoke for the last time in the East Room of the White House and went to his memoir, RN: A Memoir given to me as a gift by him when I was installed as the 48th Minister in Line of Succession since 1628 at the Collegiate Church and read the words that he shared with staff and friends that day in August 1974:

We think sometimes when things happen that don't go the right way; we think that when you don't pass the bar exam the first time – I happened to, but I was just lucky; I mean, my writing was so poor the bar examiner said, "We have just got to let the guy through." We think that when someone dear to us dies, we think that when we lose an election, we think that when we suffer a defeat, that all is ended. We think, as TR said, that the light had left his life forever.

Not true, It is only a beginning, always. The young must know it; the old must know it. It must always sustain us, because the greatness comes not when things go always good for you, but the greatness comes and you are really tested when you take some knocks, some disappointments, when sadness comes, because only if you have been in the deepest valley can you ever know how magnificent it is to be on the highest mountain...

always give your best, never get discouraged, never be petty; always remember, others may hate you, but those who hate you don't win unless you hate them, and then you destroy yourself.

Fifteen years later after these words were shared with those gathered in the East Room of the White House and the millions who observed his last speech as President of the United States, I was standing with Richard Nixon in his private office, wondering who told him that day as he resigned the Presidency, "Are you going to let this defeat you?" Certainly the circumstances of his life, internally and externally, could have resulted in a more tragic demise. Fortunately, in looking back at his Quaker roots and the profound influence of his grandmother's and mother's faith, he was able to see the power of that simple, firm belief of "Peace at the Center." Peace at the core. Peace at the center of the soul. Peace that was greater than all our sin. Peace that was greater than any circumstance, like cancer, that would eat away at every cell in our body.

It baffled my mind, standing there in prayer with Richard Nixon, my uncle and family. Such peace is often very clearly understood. There are other aspects of that peace, which will far surpass our comprehension, our understanding. This is why that peace is called a grace of our undeserving. It defies the mind.

Each of us has to find our peace from within. And if it is to be "real" it must be unaffected by circumstances.

Most heartily then, I pray for people like Barack Obama, his wife Michelle and their two girls. Most heartily I pray for people like George and Laura Bush, who daily we are reminded on MSNBC, that it is so many days since the previous President announced "mission accomplished" in Iraq.

The rest of the petition in the Book of Common Prayer says:

We humbly entreat thee also for all sorts and conditions of people; that thou wouldst be pleased to make thy ways known unto them, thy saving health unto all nations. May it please thee to preserve all that travel by land, air, or water, to succor all that are in peril or need; and to satisfy the wants of all thy creatures. We also commend to thy goodness all those who are in any way afflicted or distressed, in mind, body, or estate; that it may please thee to comfort and relieve them according to their several necessities, giving them patience under their sufferings, and a happy issue out of all their afflictions.

Whether for Presidents or for all sorts and conditions of people we encounter every day of our life, I think it would profit our own souls and well-being, if we keep our minds focused and grounded, *Still, in One Peace*. For we know full well, as it is in our own lives, as in the lives of others, that the external and internal circumstances are more than enough for any of us to handle. I do not want to be a negative, harmful, hateful, vengeful or mean-spirited influence in any person's life. I do not want to contribute to their already wounded spirits or broken lives. I'd rather hold them by the hand or in my thoughts, and together be *Still, in One Peace*. In such moments, we help others find that peace within, as we deal with our external and internal circumstances. As we fill the world with love that results in others finding happiness that can issue out of all their afflictions and disappointments.

Resource: *RN, The Memoirs of Richard Nixon*, Grosset and Dunlap, New York, 1978

The Book of Common Prayer, The Seabury Press, 1977

Chapter Six

Detachment

The soul that is attached to anything, however much good there may be in it, will not arrive at the liberty of divine union. For whether it be a strong wire rope or a slender and delicate thread that holds the bird, it matters not, if it really holds it fast; for, until the cord be broken, the bird cannot fly.
St. John of the Cross

One who would be serene and pure needs but one thing, detachment.
Meister Eckhart

This week in New York City a 48-year-old woman was killed by a subway train, after jumping onto the tracks to retrieve her handbag she accidentally dropped. Bystanders screamed as the train approached, while she frantically attempted to climb back onto the platform. Frozen in fear, she was crushed to death. The picture on the front pages of the New York newspapers, showed her handbag, held by transit agents and police officers. The bag contained her gym clothes and CP. She risked her life for clothing and her Blackberry. Riding the subway this morning I read the ad: "Your life is worth more than your belongings – If you drop something onto the tracks summon a booth agent or policeman." A life lost over two pieces of clothing and a technological gadget. Sometimes grasping onto things makes us lose all sense of rationale.

The soul that is attached to *anything,* **anything,** however much good there may be in it, will not arrive at the liberty of divine union.

When attached to any *one thing,* that obsession becomes our idol. Our god. We cannot be attached to any one entity and expect to *arrive* at the liberty of divine union. We are made prisoner to that attachment. We might strive for that harmony, but attachment to any one thing, no matter how much good it affords, will make us fall short of complete, spiritual attainment. When we are possessed by things, we are entrapped by them. Imprisoned by them. Controlled and manipulated by them. And in the case of this woman on the New York City subway platform, we are destroyed by them. A strong wire rope hold or a slender delicate thread can attach us to a false sense of security. The attainment of serenity and purity of spirit will elude us. There can only be "the liberty of divine union," the freedom in that One accord, when we place our lives in the stillness of that One peace. Not in our attachment to things or to that one "cord" from which we receive our false identity.

A story of a Monk and a traveler clearly reveals the hold that "things" have upon us and how "things" prevent us from attaining that divine union, until we realize that the attainment of "things" is no guarantee of inner fulfillment or happiness.

A monk in his travels once found a precious stone and kept it. One day he met a traveler, and when the monk opened his bag to share his provisions with him, the traveler saw the jewel and asked the monk to give it to him. The monk did so readily. The traveler departed, overjoyed with the unexpected gift of the precious stone that was enough to give him wealth and security for the rest of his life. However, a few days later he came back in search of the monk, found him, gave him back the stone, and entreated him, 'Now give me something much more precious than this stone, valuable as it is. Give me that which enabled you to give it to me.'

The request the traveler makes of the monk, to be given the secure, inner peace, serenity or contentment that the monk possesses, is something the traveler has been searching for, but which he was willing to forfeit for a fleeting sense of security. Peering into the Monk's bag he coveted all that sparkles, glitters, all that is gold and costly. In a few short days, he was still wandering around, with a valuable gem in his pocket, but with emptiness in his spirit and soul. He still found himself deprived of serenity. The gem was contaminating his soul, because, the attachment to this precious jewel was in actuality a possession that was adulterating the more desirable quality of his own life, a purer quality that was being impaired by possessions, things, that held him like a wire rope and slender thread.

We must be freed from anything that adulterates, taints and impairs. The subway rider, who lost her life, was impaired in her thinking. Things can adulterate our lives. No matter if we are wearing Hope Diamonds, driving the most expensive cars, residing in multimillion dollar homes and apartments, sailing our yachts, or fitting ourselves in expensive designer clothes, all these "things and attachments" cannot compare to the value of who we are as human beings. They offer no lasting benefit. We cling to them and permit ourselves to be tainted, adulterated and impaired by their delusion. We contaminate our truer, deeper selves, and like that bird, whether through slender thread, or wire rope, we are suppressed by them and cannot fly until we can free our grasp from them, allowing ourselves to find the serene, pure place of life, where we can be free and *Still, in One Peace*. Until we release those attachments, we won't be free in that divine union. Free to find our place where we can be *Still, in One Peace*. In one accord, with the One, who gives us our truest peace.

Chapter Seven

The Unstirred Mind/Snow Globes

When the mind is completely still, unstirred even in its depths, we see straight through to the ground of our being.
Eknath Kaswaran

Perhaps every home at one time has had a snow globe, or snow dome, those miniature decorative paperweights sold as novelties or personalized gifts. Snow globes contain tiny flakes of white plastic to simulate a snow fall whenever they are shaken. Some contain glitter, or shapes of musical notes or colored confetti. The snow cascades over a holiday scene, family photographs or popular tourist sites.

"Snow globes were developed in Europe during the latter 17th century and were made from leaded glass formed into the shape of a dome. The scenes were of detailed and well-crafted scenes of castles or famous cities. The expensive process of molding leaded glass for snow globes was finally replaced by inexpensive, thinner glass and today are molded out of impressionable plastic, but nevertheless remain popular souvenir items". We vigorously jiggle them and watch the snowflakes drift and swirl around the dome until the flakes come to settle on the base of the dome. (History of Snowglobes/Internet).

While the snowflakes create a magical and mystical scene as they flutter about, I am reminded that the globe is designed for the purpose of creating the enchanted image, or framing a treasured picture of a loved one, by shaking and "stirring" the water within the globe creating the blizzard-like effect, which within moments settles as soft snow fallen upon the base of the molded glass, only to be vigorously shaken repeatedly, keeping the magic swirling before our eyes.

In its design, the globe is filled with just enough flakes to create the charming scene, without distorting the visibility of the image encased within the globe. We continue to shake the dome to enjoy the tranquil falling of gentle snowflakes.

Our mind is often like these snow globes, shaken and stirred, preventing us from seeing clearly or finding our way through the blinding storms of our lives. When we fail to settle down our minds, stop fretting and worrying, everything becomes blurred. We lose our sense of direction and inner tranquility.

When we look with our sense of sight into a clear sky, we perceive in a dark night the sea of stars in the vast universe. During daylight, we see the universe from an earth suspended among planetary splendor as we stare into infinity.

But our ground of being is not *something* or *someone* "out there." When the mind is completely still, unstirred even in its depth, we see straight through to the ground of our being. Straight through to something *within us*.

We know that if our brain was exposed during an autopsy procedure, we would look at our own brain and realize the constraints and confines of its size, housed in the defined structure of the skull, encapsulated in our cranium. We would know our finiteness.

What gives the mind its infinite sense of imagination and dimension? What gives it its vision to dream unimaginable possibilities and surprises, when we know its restricted dimensions defined by a knitted skull around its soft tissues? It must be something that enables us to see beyond the confines of the cranium. That allows us to see straight through to the ground of our being. What is it that gives us the infinity within, though we are finite in our bodily design?

The soul! The ground of our being. We might be able to look up at the stars, but we can only reach them by knowing that indeed what we glance upon in some far distant stratosphere, resides within the soul. It is the soul that connects us to the stars, or carries us to the heavens. Into the depths of infinity. We find that that universe is not something that we are a part of. We find that that universe is something within us. If we can but still the mind, we will see it, straight through to the ground of our being. In our soul. If we are still, unstirred, we will find ourselves *Still, in One Peace.*

It is the soul that gives the mind its depth perception and the heart its broad and ever flowing streams of love and joy. It is the soul that opens the mind to imagined possibility. The soul that allows the mind to question why! Or the eyes to see. Or the heart to feel. We might see with our eyes into infinity, but what we see must be brought into the depth of our soul, in order for what we see to be interpreted into what we feel. What we feel, gives meaning and essence to what we see.

We might see stars with our eyes, but our lives only travel to distant places of our imaginings, not through our sight, but through our soul. Without the soul, it's just a blank stare, which happens to be able to see beyond the stars. Our hearts might be inspired by words of love or music of inspiration, but it is only the soul, the depth of our being, that will embrace those words, share those words. It is only the soul that will become the music itself, the harmony within our self-contained, defined bodies. Otherwise, sound or music are just vibrations against our skin. It is the soul that makes the heart sing. That makes our bodies instruments of praise and music.

If we are completely still, if the mind is completely still, even in its depth, we see straight through to the ground of our being. If I am moved by Rachmaninov's *Adagio* from *Symphony Number 2* it is not that I am moved because I happen to be listening to it. Just listening to it, I would be merely listening to notes printed on a staff, in symphonic form, played by an orchestra. I am moved, because, if my mind, my senses, and my hearing is still enough to be attuned to its stirring emotional strains, then, and only then, does that music flow through my senses, into my mind, which flows it straight to the depth of my being – my soul. Otherwise, it remains only like elevator music in a crowded, chatter-filled corporate skyscraper, and I catch a note, here and there among the clamor and fast-paced business of an exhausting day, running to or from work.

A mind that continues to stay stirred and troubled will never see through to the ground of its being. If we are still, we will see straight through the heart, the mind, the eye, the ear, the nerve endings, the blood vessels, the skin layers, straight through to the ground of our being. To the soul, where in that still place we will find ourselves in the ground of our One peace. Straight through to the One, who is our inner peace.

When I step into the ocean at my summer home on a day when the sea is like a placid lake without a ripple, and the waters move unstirred by roaring waves, I can wade to depths in the water where I stand with the water to my neck in the crystal clear reflections of the sea. Standing still, looking down, I count my ten toes, see the ripple of the sand with their ribbon-like design patterned by the soft, flowing ocean currents, spot a tiny sand crab or watch a darting school of fish; when the water is unstirred I see clearly through to the ground where my feet are positioned on the ocean floor.

When the mind is cluttered, filled with the sediments of daily concerns, or clogged with built-up plaque of a lifetime of unresolved anger, resentments, bitterness, fear, disappointments, worries, anxieties, battering me like tossing waves, it becomes increasingly complex to see through that mind, straight through to the ground of my being, especially if I allow those things to constantly be stirred and shaken in my mind. My psyche stays troubled, my mind shaken feverishly like a snow globe.

When my mind stays distressed, the soul stays cast down, under the invariable burden of fretful apprehension that swirls around my brain like unrelenting blizzard snowfalls that drift into the corners of my mind trapping me in their mounting accumulation. Literally, I'm buried under them and my way is obscured by the impaired visibility, unable to see my way through or to create a clear path. Many of the Vancouver Winter Olympic 2010 competitions were postponed because of the snowfall conditions on Whistle Mountain that made it difficult for the skiers to see the run or for the judges to observe the athletes. The competitions were suspended until the swirling snows diminished or ceased.

It is important that we place our troubled spirit into places of quietness. Places of rest. In still waters. Perfect peace. In that One place of rest and peace. Mary Rowles Jarvis wrote:

Not in the turmoil of the raging storm,
Not in the earthquake or devouring flame;
But in the hush that could all fear transform,
The still, small whisper to the prophet came.

O Soul, keep silence on the mount of God,
Though cares and needs throb around you like a sea;
From prayers, petitions, and desires unshod,
Be still, and hear what God will say to thee.

All fellowship has interludes of rest,
New strength maturing in each level of power;
The sweetest Alleluias of the blest
Are silent, for the space of half an hour.

O rest, in utter quietude of soul,
Abandon words, leave prayer and praise awhile;
Let your whole being, hushed in His control,
Learn the full meaning of His voice and smile.

Not as an athlete wrestling for a crown,
Not taking Heaven by violence of will;
But with your Father as a child sit down,
And know the bliss that follows His "Be Still!?

(from Streams in the Desert, LB Cowan, Zondervan, 1997)

When the mind is completely still, unstirred even in its depths, we will find ourselves **Still, in One Peace**, and see straight through to the One who is the ground of our being.

Chapter Eight

The Piano/Idols

At night I think of my piano in its ocean grave. Down there everything is still and silent – there is a silence where no sound may be under the deep, deep sea.
From the movie, The Piano.

My will has chosen life!
From the movie, The Piano

Due to the increase of suicides, especially among teenagers, on the Tappan Zee Bridge that crosses the Hudson River in New York, the Port of Authority placed signs at both the entrance of the roadway to the bridge and the apex of the suspension over the turbulent currents of the river. The signs simply read, "Your Life Is Worth Living!" including a phone number to encourage desperate individuals to seek help. The signpost was installed following a week when three teenagers jumped from the bridge.

At the height of the 2008 economic crisis in America, a number of high profile bankers and entrepreneurs ended their lives. Their self-worth had been attached to, what Jim Keller, minister of Redeemer Presbyterian Church in New York City in his book *Counterfeit gods* claimed, "their money." Their wealth became their counterfeit god. When they lost it, they found no reason to live.

What happens when we lose the very thing to which we identify our self-worth? To the things we have made into our personal gods? Do we fall to pieces? Do we end our lives? Or do we, by some miraculous circumstance, emerge from that turmoil, if only in one piece, though fragile, shattered, bruised and emotionally wounded?

The movie *The Piano,* starring Holly Hunter is an emotionally riveting testament to one who eventually let go of the very idol, her piano, to which she had attached her identity and love, but not before that idol would swallow her and plunge her to an ocean grave.

Actress Holly Hunter won an Academy Award for her portrayal of a "self-willed mute who becomes the imported bride of land grabber Stewart in the recently colonized New Zealand wilderness of Victorian times."

When Ada McGrath, played by Hunter, and her daughter Flora, played by a young Anna Pacquin (who also won an Academy Award for her portrayal as the strong-willed young daughter) arrived in New Zealand, she brings along with them her treasured piano which her new husband refused to carry home with them, leaving it to stand silently on the sandy shore, as the rising tide creeps closer, swirling around the piano legs, threatening to destroy the fine wooden instrument, leaving it like a splintered shipwreck among the rocks.

Because of the abandonment of her adored piano, Ada immediately detests her new husband's cruelness. We witness their intense resentment, hatred and abusive relationship.

Watching her retreat further into her isolated world of silence, Stewart acquiesces, allowing his overseer, George Baines, to retrieve the piano and house it in his cabin. George Baines becomes enamored with Ada and agrees to eventually return the piano to her if she consents to give him lessons. The instruction becomes a series of clandestine sexually charged encounters.

The Piano is a story of rage and desire centered on the music of the piano, as Ada's world becomes totally absorbed in the instrument. It is a story of deeply hidden sensuality, disguised tenderness and oppressive anger and violence. Critics called the movie, "A Greek tragedy of the Outback, complete with a Greek chorus of Maori tribesmen and a blithely uncaring natural environment that envelops the characters like an additional player."

Holly Hunter speaks her passion and sensuality through her silence. As her hands travel across the keyboard of her beloved piano, we descend into her soulful cry for love and affection.

As Ada and Baines continue their liaison, and fall in love, the strong-willed Flora discovers them in the passionate embrace of their heated sexual expression as she peers through the cracks of the cabin walls. She divulges the infidelity to her stepfather, Stewart, whose savage rage is unleashed against Ada. He drags her from the house to a wood chopping tree stump where he proceeds to cut off one of her fingers with an axe, driving the final wedge of hatred between them. Stewart eventually resigns himself to Baines and Ada's devotion.

The tribesmen escort them from the enclave through the muddy forest terrain, carrying the beloved piano which they struggle to position and secure on the boat as it precariously rests on the edges of the catamaran, threatening the safety of the passengers as it begins to sail across the rising waves.

Through her expressive glances and body language, she watches the fearful concern of those on board. She suggests having the piano tossed overboard. Though the crew is willing to sail on, she persists. The piano is slowly pushed over the edge, into the swelling waves, and disappears beneath the surface of the sea, as a huge rope attached securely to the piano begins to rapidly uncoil as the piano descends to the ocean floor.

At Ada's feet the mound of rope swiftly uncurls. She watches the piano descend beneath the waves. In her horrified gaze, she makes the decision to place her foot into the unwinding rope that snaps her leg, pulling her overboard. Together, Ada and her beloved piano descend into the silent depths of the sea. She chooses to end her life and join her piano in the silent abyss.

In the depths of the dark, murky sea, we watch Ada's fearful eyes as she gasps for breath, and air escapes from her compressed mouth as water fills her lungs. As the air bubbles diminish, we wince and grieve over her choice to end her life.

As decisively as she had placed her foot into the contraction of the rope, she begins to struggle against the weight of the submerging piano and its tethered hold on her life. We realize that she has a change of heart. We wonder in her fight to now alter her descent, whether her attempt to survive is futile.

She begins to frantically use her free foot to dislodge her trapped foot from the web of death. Finally unbound, she rises to the surface where she is retrieved, and laid lifeless upon the catamaran floor.

In the closing scene of the movie, time has passed and Ada, Flora and Baines are gathered in the living room of their home. Hunter is playing a piano, assisted by the prosthetic finger that Baines crafted from metal and leather, attached around the stump of her amputated finger.

We hear the thoughts of her mind, as she plays the new piano: "At night I think of my piano in its ocean grave. Down there everything is still and silent. There is a silence where no sound may be under the deep, deep sea." The voice of her idol was silenced in its deep ocean grave.

The movie ends with Ada's words, "My will has chosen life."

While the piano resides in its silent grave, Ada has found life in the Still, silence of One peace and hope, wherein lies the new music she creates with her liberated spirit, no longer imprisoned by the idol that could have entombed her in its ocean grave, but liberated to create the joy and music that she found in the Still place of peace within her heart. In her heart where she found the will to choose life.

She realized life was worth living. She had been willing to forfeit her life, for the piano, her counterfeit god. A god that almost destroyed her.

But a new song, one not played on the keyboard of a piano, but on the still, centered place of her heartstrings, made her realize the significance of her life, the power of love and the deep desire to live.

She was free of the idol that once held her, liberated by the love that now enfolded her. She had chosen life. In choosing life, she found that her life was *Still, in One Peace*. She survived the death of her idol god – the beloved piano. In her newfound peace, she brought music from her heart into her hands, through her fingers, as imperfect as her hand now was, and made her piano play its unending song of love.

The real music was no longer in the piano; it was in the music of her heart, a heart in which she found herself *Still, in One Peace*.

Life is worth living! We can have the will to choose life! To find life. To be *Still, in One Peace*. Which idols must we abandon first?

MoviePhonePlots/Internet/The Piano

Chapter Nine

A Mind That Is Still Is Divine

In the rush and noise of life as you have intervals, step home within yourself and be still. Wait upon God, and feel his presence; this will carry you evenly through your day's business.
Anonymous

One's action ought to come out of an achieved stillness: not to be mere rushing on.
D. H. Lawrence

A mind that is fast is sick.
A mind that is slow is sound
A mind that is still is divine
Meher Baba

Often in the rush and noise of life we need to get away from it all. I'm not talking about retreats, weekend vacations or extended excursions. We need a breathing place for the soul, right where we are, in the middle of our exhausting daily routine. Just an "interval" in time where we can gather our wits about us and center down in some calming moment of peacefulness and serenity.

It is laughable to think that in the rush of our work routines that a 15-minute break in the morning, and a time for respite in the afternoon, at the water cooler or coffee station, is enough to replenish our spirit and revitalize our energy. No wonder the local corner deli displays at the cash register counter, those Energy Shot bottles to provide a quick surge of adrenaline to our weary bodies. We are willing to consume power drinks like Bawls Energy Drink, Five Hour Energy Drink, Who's Your Daddy

Energy Drink, Tab Energy, Red Bull, Monster Energy, many of which have 200 mil of caffeine, or Guarana, two to three times more caffeine than coffee, all for the purpose of getting a real power kick. But we find very little time to quiet down our lives, to empower them by immersing ourselves in stillness. We not only live crazed, rat race lives, but we take these drinks that allow caffeine to keep our nerves on edge, as we cram all night for exams, or attempt to keep up our stamina on the treadmill.

The pressures we face in a fast forward world are tremendous. Just look at the prediction of population trends. In 1959 there were 3 billion inhabitants on earth. In 1999 there were six billion. It is predicted that in 2045 there will be 9 billion people on our planet. (US Census Data Base). New Blackberrys and iPhones that hit the market today will be obsolete in three months. Crowded subways, congested buses, endless lines of merging traffic at turnpike toll booths, frenzied crowds at Time Square corners crossing thoroughfares against the light, halting traffic, angering drivers who pay no attention to the posted signs threatening fines for blaring their horns.

Life is a continual harassment. Piled on top of all this is the deadline to be met, multi-tasking projects to be completed before punching the clock, or the unexpected demand by supervisors that we stay after hours or work on our scheduled day off. Then there are the management details of home, the care of children, cooking the meals, doing the laundry, cleaning the apartment, and the endless chores and projects that preoccupy our lives on days off and distract us from finding a morsel of peace that participating in our spiritual life centers might provide on Jewish Sabbaths on Friday evenings, or worship at Saturday evening or Sunday morning church services. Our fast pace, rat race driven lives, divert us from the source of inner strength and renewal. We make no time, achieve no interval, for being still, in God's presence. The rat race convinces us that we've got to paint the house, wash the car, do the loads of laundry, on what we call our "days off" from all the hectic rat race routines. We might be home from work on a Saturday or Sunday, but we still are unable to step home, within ourselves.

In the rush and noise of the day, as you have intervals, step home within yourself. Often, we just can't find the "intervals" to step into those still, quiet places.

There seems to be nothing that can carry us "evenly" through the course of a day. We just can't find that "interval" space, that quiet moment, those somatic sleep moments that can rejuvenate our bodies and replenish our emotional stamina. We are unable to step into ourselves and find that still, quiet place. There is nothing to carry us evenly through the day. Some of us have three- and four-hour commuting days, getting up at the crack of dawn to drive to the parking lots to car pool or catch express buses into the city, returning home at night at seven-thirty, eight o'clock, turning out the lights at ten pm only to begin the ritual again at five am.

"The constant rat race in which we live really has nothing to do with current trends, lifestyles, mass media growth, technological advancements or the rapid increase of knowledge." It has everything to do with our human nature, that finds it difficult to nurture those breathing places for the soul, those places, where we can step inside, and be at home in the still, quiet assurances of solitude and peace. We exhaust ourselves by daily activities and responsibilities and find ourselves barely surviving in one piece.

Blaise Pascal said that "all miseries derive from not being able to sit quietly in a room alone." We can not only sit quietly in a room alone, but find that we foster misery in our lives when we are unable to find one brief interval in a single day, to *step inside of ourselves,* to be at home with ourselves, and in that internal stillness to find that breathing place for our soul where we wait on God, feel His presence and allow that presence to carry us *evenly* through the day.

Meher Baba said, "the mind that is fast is sick." We need to learn to be slow. To be still. When we do, our minds will become sound. They will discover something divine about being **Still, in that One Peace**. D. H. Lawrence said, "One's action ought to come out of an achieved stillness: not to be mere rushing on." Stillness, that breathing place for the soul, must be nurtured out of an action of **achieved** stillness. This stillness is something that requires an effort on our part to achieve it. It just will not happen. We must be intentional in making those "intervals" an achieved part of our daily strategy. Without it, our minds will remain sick, our strength will be depleted and our resilience washed-out.

Lewis Carroll, in **Alice in Wonderland**, whose wonderful story has recently been retold in Tim Burton's cinematic triumph starring Johnny Depp, speaks very directly to the fast paced, hectic lives we live. The dialogue between Alice and the Queen is quite revealing about the way we continue to "run" through life:

Alice never could quite make out, in thinking it over after-wards, how it was that they began. All she remembers is that they were running hand in hand, and the Queen went so fast that it was all she could do to keep up with her; and still the Queen kept saying, "Faster! Faster!" but Alice felt she could not go faster, though she had no breath left to say so.

The most curious part of the thing was that the trees and other things round them never changed their places at all; however fast Alice and the Queen went, they never seemed to pass anything. "I wonder if all the things move along with us?" thought poor, puzzled Alice. And the Queen seemed to guess her thoughts, for she cried, "Faster! Don't try to talk!"

Not that Alice had any idea of doing that. She felt as if she would never be able to talk again, she was getting so much out of breath; and still the Queen cried "Faster!" and dragged her along. "Are we nearly there?" Alice managed to pant out at last.

"Nearly there?" the Queen repeated. "Why, we passed it ten minutes ago! Faster!" And they ran on for a time in silence, with the wind whistling in Alice's ears and almost blowing her hair off her head.

"Now, Now?" cried the Queen. "Faster! Faster!" And they went so fast that at last they seemed to skim through the air, hardly touching the ground with their feet, till suddenly, just as Alice was getting quite exhausted, they stopped, and she found herself sitting on the ground, breathless and giddy. The Queen said, "You may rest a little now."

Alice looked around her in great surprise. "Why, I do believe we've been under this tree the whole time? Everything's just as it was!"

"Of course it is," said the Queen; "What would you have it?" "Well, in our country," said Alice, still panting a little, "you'd generally get to somewhere else, if you ran very fast for a long time as we've been doing."

"A slow sort of country!" said the Queen. "Now, here you see, it takes all the running you can do, to keep in the same place. If you want to get somewhere else you must run at least twice as fast as that!"

We live hectic lives at a rapid pace. We live rat race lifestyles and get nowhere. We get nowhere *fast*.

The point is very clear in the sped-up world in which we live. In the rush and noise of life, as you have intervals, step home within yourself and be still. This must be an achieved, intentionally designed plan for your life every day. The mind that is fast is sick. The mind that is slow is sound. The mind that is still is divine.

Make an interval today.

Step home within yourself. Into God's presence.

Be *Still, in One Peace*. It will be the only thing that will carry you evenly through your day's business. The actions of your life will then be achieved out of that stillness, rather than your actions, keeping you merely rushing on in your frenzied life, causing you to find yourself sitting under that same tree, having gotten nowhere, fast. Life is not to be lived merely rushing on. A song reminds us to "Stop and Smell the Roses."

Stop. Create an achieved stillness for your life.

A life that is still is divine.

Resource: US Census Report and Data Base

Alice's Adventures in Wonderland, Lewis Carroll, MacMillian, United Kingdom, November 26, 1865

Chapter Ten

The Real One Can't Be Expressed in Words

If there's something that occupies writers and poets of the spiritual life, it is certainly the effect of silence. They stress that silence is the space where the mysteries between God and humanity have a chance to come to light.

Moments of true compassion will remain engraved on our hearts as long as we live. Often these are moments without words: moments of deep silence.

Silence makes us attentive to God's word. The word of God penetrates through the thick of human verbosity to the silent center of the heart; silence opens in us the space where the word can be heard. Without silence, the word loses its re-creative power.

If it is true that God is greater than the human heart then God is certainly greater than the words that human beings – no matter how inspired they may be – have spoken about the Eternal One.

Language possesses a tension that cannot prove the Real One, for the Real One cannot be captured in words.

Henri Nouwen

Silence
Space
Mystery
"Be Still and Know that I am God."
Being Still, In One Peace
is to

move from a mind of inquisitiveness
to a heart of attentiveness
to a soul of openness
a soul that is Still, in One peace
without words
for in this place of silence, we find the One who dwells in
   peace
where we have no words
to bring that One to the center of our being
Only stillness, quietness, invites the mystery...
reveals the light.

The thickness of my verbosity... The One comes to dwell in the
   silence of my mind without words, breaking through the
   density of thought
where light
reveals its peace.

In that silence the word finds its re-creative power.
"That which fills the heart also pours out of the mouth"

Time to write again!
Words... from the silent center flow
in my attempt to prove the Real One.

Chapter Eleven

God between our Faith and Circumstances

Faith puts God between itself and its circumstances and looks at them through Him.
Anonymous

Sometimes we get so trapped and entangled in our circumstances that we cannot elude the injury and harm they cause.

Often these conditions are not of our making or choosing. It is not a question of finding ourselves in the wrong place at the wrong time. Not one of us is safe from the circumstances that occur unexpectedly and indiscriminately. "It has nothing to do with fate, or the cards we are dealt. And if we do dodge them, it has nothing to do with the luck of the draw."

When circumstances cause injury and harm, we can at least put ourselves in the Still, One place of peace, so that faith can put God between itself and our circumstances allowing us to look at our conditions through Him.

This will only happen if we place ourselves *Still, in One Peace*. Resting still, in our faith, and finding peace in our circumstances, as we look at them through God, the One in the center of our peace. The God who holds us in the firm promise of love and peace.

My Uncle Richard and his four sons, my cousins, Richard, Edward, David and Robert are commercial fishermen who run their business from the docks of Belford, New Jersey, near the Atlantic Highlands region of Sandy Hook, New Jersey. I have been mesmerized by their stories of fishing off the Atlantic coastline. On several occasions I joined them on the decks of their ships as they chartered the waters in search of fish.

In reading about the life of commercial fisherman, I

discovered an interesting insight and analogy of fishing as it pertains to the circumstances we encounter in life, circumstances that trap, harm and injure us.

In the backyard of their homes located along the creeks and tributaries of the fishing co-op where they slip their three ships, mounds of nets are stretched for cleaning and repair. These are the nets that they have been able to maintain.

There are other nets that have been cut and discarded in the deep seas, because they have become entangled on rocks and crags, or snarled on submerged debris or wreckage beneath the ocean surface. It is these nets that have become circumstantial threats and harmful to marine life.

They are known as *"ghost nets!"*

Fishing boat operators often cut loose snagged nets and get their boats free, so that they can resume their search for fish or return to port. The "derelict nets" remain where they were snagged, often for years, catching and killing marine life.

The Northwest Straits foundation estimates that derelict gill nets capture and kill an estimated 30,000 marine birds, 110,000 fish and 2 million invertebrates, like crabs, annually over and area of 645 acres of Puget Sound marine habitats. The foundation reports that since 2001, the Derelict Removal Project has removed 1,300 gill nets covering 280 acres.

These ghost nets equal death for marine life. According to the U.S. National Oceanic and Atmospheric Administration (NOAA), abandoned nets float aimlessly throughout the ocean.

Discarded nets pose a great threat to the life of the sea. Their synthetic materials decay slowly. The ocean cannot break down their plastic or nylon fibers, so they can drift for years, indiscriminately through the waters.

The study shows that the nets continue to fish, as they drift. No marine animal is safe. The ghost nets trap turtles, birds, and fish. In one article written in *Live Science*, "divers freed 170 endangered Hawaiian monk seals from ghost nets in the last decade. Turtles and fish, view the floating masses as food and shelter sources. The nets go unperceived, making them a deadly form of pollution."

All forms of sea life can become entangled in marine debris. Entanglement leads to suffocation, starvation, drowning, increased vulnerability to predators. Marine debris can constrict an entangled animal's movement which results in exhaustion or development of an infection from deep wounds caused by tightening material.

But the impact and damage is not limited to mobile animals. Plants, immobile living organisms, and sensitive ecosystems can all be harmed by ghost nets. Coral reefs are damaged by discarded fishing gear that breaks or suffocates coral. Plants are smothered by plastic bags and fishing nets.

Totally unaware of the threat from the ghost nets, marine life swims innocently in their environment, and in the dark abyss of the waters, or in their search for food, they become entrapped and entangled by no choice of their own. We have seen the skins of whales and seals, gouged with deep wounds from the tightening nylon nets around their struggling bodies.

Some things happen to us in life that harm, entangle, threaten our lives or even result in our deaths and severe illnesses and debilitating diseases. These are circumstances we have no control over. They come into our lives as ghost nets. We become entangled in them. We struggle to survive. To set ourselves free from them. Many times we cannot liberate ourselves from these circumstances. They cripple and harm us. But if we put God in between our faith and our circumstances and look at them through Him, we might be able to discern a deeper meaning in the blessings for our growth that these circumstances might provide. The nets that have been cast into the ocean depths have harmed marine life. When we find ourselves in this type of circumstance, we can "cast our burdens, cares, pains, sorrows, wounds and despair, on the One who reminds us that we are His charge." The familiar story of the little fish highlights the presence of the One who is around us in all our circumstances:

There was a fish that lived a perfectly normal life in the ocean until one day he looked down into its depths and saw the vast space below him. He began to worry about falling into that deep, black abyss. The little fish began to chase his tail, reasoning that if he could catch it with his mouth he could hold it up and thus keep from falling. As he chased his tail he became hysterical. Finally, the wise old ocean asked him why he was making all those gyrations. The fish said that he was trying to catch his tail to keep from falling. The ocean said:
Listen little fish, I'm the ocean. You live in me. I am above you, below you, in you, and about you. I feed you, sustain you, supply you with air, and, look, while you have been listening to me talk; you have forgotten to chase your tail. You are doing all right. Forget yourself and live in me.
(Adapted from Barrel Berg by Clarence J. Forsberry, The Ministers Manual 1975). Harper and Row, p 261.)

There are ghost nets drifting everywhere:

Go to work one morning and receive a pink slip. The company is downsizing.

Go to the doctor's office – you're diagnosed with a terminal illness. The ghost net tightens around your mind and body that is struggling to be free or hoping to find, in a second opinion, more encouraging news.

Your partner or spouse leaves you unexpectedly! You're blind-sided by the news that they are in love with someone else. The ghost net of rejection snarls all your dreams and hopes. How are you going to pay all the bills? Reassure the children? Hold the family together?

We can list all the devastating ghost nets and circumstances. If you are reading this, you have a list of your own circumstances.

In order to find some meaning out of them, we must place ourselves intentionally in a certain place.

FAITH (our Stillness) THE ONE (we call God). OUR CIRCUMSTANCES.

Faith allows us to look at our circumstances through the One, who helps us find peace in all our circumstances, no matter what happens to us because of our circumstances. Our state of affairs doesn't have to cause us to crumble in pieces.

When Faith allows us to see our circumstances through the One who is our lasting peace, no matter when the ghost nets might appear, we do not have to remain entangled or entrapped in them. We can be held, be still, in the promise of One peace.

When you are gyrating, swirling in the circles of despair, trying to catch your tail, just to hold yourself up, look at your circumstance through God, and you will see that God is the One, still presence in whom no ghost nets can harm you. The One in whom is your lasting peace. The One who holds you up.

Resource: Northwest Straights Foundation: Ghostnets; US National Oceanic Atmospheric Administration

Chapter Twelve

The Rhythm of Music and the Silence More Musical than Song

I know that eight notes in each octave and the varieties of rhythm offer me opportunities that all of human genius will never exhaust.
Igor Stravinsky

Silence, more musical than any song.
Christina Rossetti

My idea is that there is music in the air, music all around us, the world is full of music and you simply take as much as you require.
Sir Edward Elgar

There is a wonderful scene in the movie *My Life in Ruins*, that reveals how music can bring our thoughts to a still place, freezing within our minds the panorama of life that music allows us to perceive. The romantic comedy is the sequel, but not continuing the story of *My Big Fat Greek Wedding*, a movie block-buster starring Nia Vardalos. In *My Life in Ruins*, Nia plays Georgia, a history professor turned travel guide, who is assigned to a substandard tour bus, driven by a young, grungy Greek, Alexis Giorgoulis, who plays the part of Poopi, who helps Georgia discover the "kefi," the "passion" within her heart. Georgia is discouraged and disenchanted that her tour group is more concerned about shopping, ice cream and swims in the Aegean water than they are in having a passion for antiquity.

Nia asks the critical question of her bus driver Poopi, a question she eventually confronts herself: "What are you doing with your life, Poopi?" As the story unfolds among the breath-taking landscapes of Greece, a transformation begins to take place in the lives of the sightseers on the dilapidated bus and within the hearts of Georgia and the bus driver. Circumventing her own passion, her "kefi," Georgia is unsuspecting that it is Poopi who leaves a wild flower at her seat each time they stop at an historic site. She is oblivious that she has enticed him with her heart and spirit.

While sightseeing through the rugged, winding roadways along the Aegean coastline, Georgia distracts the passengers and Poopi during one of her playful antics, as she lets down her reticence in altering her inflexibility. Distracted, Poopi loses control of the bus, narrowly escaping going over a cliff, as the tourists scream in horror. Provoked to anger he shrieks, "I could have killed you all!" As the passengers disembark, he walks to a ridge overlooking the sea. The group encourages Georgia to join him, to open her eyes and see his affection. She realizes that she has been missing the nuances of his affection.

As he contemplates the magnificent vista of the Aegean Sea, he articulates the infatuation he has for the exquisiteness he sees and how he has discovered the intensity of that fervor with each tour bus he drives throughout Greece. That pleasure is like a conductor of a symphony orchestra:

"The conductor comes out with a stick. He waves the stick. When he does I hear the most beautiful music. I hear it up close. I hear the most beautiful sounds the world has ever heard. I feel it in the bones. This is what my job is like."

"I turn the world this way and that way. Before me comes a vision. Always beautiful – the scenery is "frozen music.""

"You are too busy looking up," he says to her. "I like your passion for our history. But, look here, inside your heart. Feel it in your bones." "Find the music inside of yourself. When you do everything will be captured as "frozen music."" "And you know what?" he asks her, to which she interrupts and says, "You have the best seat in the house!"

All of us can learn to see life as "frozen music." We can capture it in our eyes, our souls, our grasp. We can hold it still, in our imagination.

As a ten-year-old child, I listened to my grandfather's large, black 78 RPM classical records which instilled within me the wonder of music to transport my mind and feelings to exciting thoughts and images, as a world of magic and imagination opened to me through symphonies that colored my imagination. I watched those 78 RPM records spinning on the turntable, pulling me like a whirlpool into the depths of the fantasies that swirled around my mind as I became absorbed in the music.

Music filled our home. When Mom played the piano, we sang many of the Broadway show tunes. Sacred music was a part of our music appreciation as well, since Mom and Dad, and Mom's sisters sang in the church choir. Sacred duets were often sung at parties or casual evenings at home.

I have a deep passion for film scores and soundtracks, those symphonic compositions that underscore love stories, dramas, documentaries and film epics.

I know when a movie is worth seeing simply because of the composer who writes the score.

Some of my favorite composers are the French musician Philippe Rombi, for his work in *Angel*, Ilan Eshkeri's loving compositions for *Young Victoria*, John Barry's broad range of human emotions found in such epic films as *The Scarlet Letter, Across the Sea of Time, Out of Africa, Somewhere in Time, Frances. Born Free.* Randy Edelman has composed a delightful, beautiful theme, Anna, for the movie *Leap Year*. The compositions of Jan Kaczmarek, from the movie *Unfaithful*, are haunting. Ennio Mariconne's vast repertoire, *The Mission, Love Affair*, Alan Silvestri's music from *Forrest Gump Suite*, Barrington Pheloung's work in *Hillary and Jackie*, Hans Zimmers' stirring music from the *House of The Spirits*, the delightful Julie theme from *Julie, Julia*, Bruno Coulais academy award nominated scores for *The Chorus*,

The Overture from *The Notebook*, by Aaron Zigman, Tennessee, from *Pearl Harbor* by Hans Zimmer, and John Newton's music from *The Prince of Tides*, the Aria from *Dawn of A New Century* by Secret Garden, *Legends of the Fall* by James Horner, are works that repeatedly stir my heart.

I love the music of Steven Schwartz from *Enchanted*, especially the love theme, *So Close*. Paul Winter's *Sun Singer* is ethereal. Randy Newman's, *Awakenings* tugs at the heart as compassion for those wounded and ill comes soaring through the music. The theme song from *Sense and Sensibility* and the lilting sounds of *Willoughby*, by Patrick Doyle and the closing credit theme of "Throw the Coins," lifts my spirit. George Fenton's, *Shadowlands*, can make me cry. Someday I'll fly Away from *Moulin Rouge*, Karl Jenkins' *Requiem and Mass of Peace*, John Goodall's score from *The Vicar of Dibly* and his memorable interpretation of *Belief* is inspiring. The lyrics of Where is it Written from the movie *Yentl*, by Alan and Marilyn Bergman, is my favorite song in which I see my own life reflected. *Tea with Mussolini*, by Alessio Olad, *The Painted Veil* and *Jane Eyre* by Alexander Displat, George Fenton's theme from *Ever After*, David Foster's "All That My Heart Can Hold," the theme song from *Shirley Valentine*, Sting's *Ocean Waltz*, Rachel Portman's *Cider House Rules*, the music of Rondo Veneziano, John Williams' theme from *Shindler's List*, the Agnes Dei from *Faure Requiem*, the *Ave Maria* sung by Inessa Galante, or Renee Fleming singing Marietta Lied from Gluck's *Korngold*, are only a few of the compositions that have allowed me to keep the frozen music in my mind.

It would take the pages of this book to list the nearly 7000 songs I have preserved on my iPod, compositions that shape my imagination. I spend hours, still, in the peace and power of music's ability to shape my understanding of life and deepen the awareness about myself. As I did during those boyhood years when I laid on my bedroom floor listening to my grandfather's 78 RPM records, I can still lay on the floor and drift into a world of "frozen images" of life. Images that become "frozen music."

On an international flight I was flying over the Italian Alps, looking out the window from the galley in the rear of the plane. Seeing the Alps from above the clouds, peering at the snow-capped mountains, the intensity of the contemplation of their beauty miles below the plane was magnified by the music of John Rutter I was listening to through my earphones. As we flew above the Alps, his song, *For The Beauty of The Earth*, brought together the visual wonder with the inner, soulful feelings that wrapped themselves around my heart as I observed the earth 35,000 feet below.

Walking along the surf at the Jersey Shore at my summer home in Ocean Grove, New Jersey, I sensed the unusual power and beauty of the pounding surf, from which danced the bright rays of the setting sun, all while listening to the composition, A Day at The Beach from the movie *Hillary and Jackie*. Or watching seagulls fly, and nestled together along the shore, the gentle winds ruffling their feathers, as I pondered Massenet's *Meditation*. Rachmaninov's *Vocalise*, can reduce me to a wet dish rag.

I remember walking in the woods, during a gentle snowfall, listening to the theme of The Pine Forest in Winter from Tchaikovsky's *Nutcracker*. I stood at the fence of my grammar school listening to the words from Madonna's song, *This Used to Be My Playground,* and was transported back to childhood days.

The music and the world around me becomes frozen in an image. I stand there, in the still, quiet reflection, looking at the scenery without any music filtering through an earphone into my senses. Just silently, at last. I feel the "still, calm, pure harmony and music inside of myself and fully understand Christina Rossetti's words, "Silence, more musical than any song." The music, the moment, the visual, the beauty, the scenery, becomes frozen music, as the music resides silently in my spirit.

Frozen Music! A still moment, in which I capture a deeper reality of the beauty of life; or ponder the significance of a person; or touch a reason and joy for living, within my own heart. Sir Edward Elgar stated clearly what I feel about the significance of music in my life, especially as it provides much of the inspiration for the varied moods of my writing and reflections:

My idea is that there is music in the air, music all around us, the world is full of music, and you simply take as much as you require.

The desire for that music is insatiable. I take as much of it as I can, and I take as much as I allow to continue to flow within my mind, heart, soul and as much as continues to solicit from me the deepest thoughts, often so trapped in my soul, only to be set free by music.

The 2009 film score written by Randy Edelman's for *Leap Year*, starring Amy Adams is simply eloquent and beautiful. The theme song, Anna's Song is written with the repetitive sequence of three notes, followed by two notes. It is music that lifts the soul, wraps it in happiness and delights one's spirit with peacefulness and tranquility, and makes me happy to be alive. It captures the pure love that Anna seeks in her romantic journey through Ireland. With the sequence of five notes, I understand the insight that Igor Stravinsky gives. It provides encouragement for me as a writer:

I know that the notes of each octave and the variety of rhythms offer me opportunities that all of human genius will never exhaust.

When talking of octaves the figure 8 springs to mind. Clarify if you mean 12 tones. This source also appears at the start of the chapter. It is the beauty of music that makes one realize that within the scope of just an octave, in writing these notes in a variety of rhythms, that I find the opportunity to write, comprehending that all of human genius will never be exhausted. This provides much encouragement when I see thousands of books in Barnes and Noble Bookstore. When I feel it a futile exercise trying to write with a new voice for the masses. The task seems insurmountable until I gain the inspiration from Stravinsky's words: that within the dimension of a musical octave exists the potential of saying something new to the world, in a way that all of human genius will never exhaust.

I recommend that you listen to Rachmaninov's Symphony Number 2, the Adagio Movement. I was introduced to this work through a gift of 50 classical CDs that my cousin Valerie gave to me for my 60th birthday. The Adagio stirred me unpredictably. It triggered deep hidden feelings and wounds, reducing me to uncontainable sobs. I told her my reaction, how the adagio touched a place of pain and hurt within my life. She wrote back with this quotation from George F. Handel:

Art thou troubled?
Music will calm thee.
Art thou weary?
Music will find you rest.
Music, source of all gladness, fill thy sadness.
Music, music ever divine.

These words affirmed, in a beautiful way everything I have felt about music all of my life:

Music calms me, brings me to a still place.

Music gives me rest, especially when life makes me weary and pain makes me fragile.

Music is the source of my gladness, even within all my sorrows it makes my sorrow to be filled with the gifts that come from taking the time, the frozen time, to feel them, to feel through them.

Music, ever divine, brings me to the One in whom I find life's true song and peace.

It is important that we live our lives in the promise and potential that music conveys in the mere scale of an octave, in a variety of rhythms, that allows us to feel and create, to live and to dream, never to exhaust the joy and meaning of life that dwelling in frozen music can provide.

Might we not imagine how profoundly life can be lived, or how our soul might soar to new realms of love and happiness and inner peace, how deeply immersed the heart can find its solitude and contentment, if we but know within the world of our own octave, in the variety of the rhythms of our experiences, that we can come to the fullness of new songs, new insights, new hopes, new dreams.

Music that calms, can allow us to rest. To make us glad.

Music, Music ever divine.

Let it fill you, still you, in the One peacefulness of its pure harmony and pure joy, and pure delight.

Be still, frozen in music. Touch the stillness that is more musical than any song or sound score.

Blaise Pascal said, "Rivers are roads which move and which carry us wither we desire to go."

So it is with music. Music is a river which moves and carries us wither we desire to go, and carries us to places deep within, where we would otherwise never travel or dare to explore.

Music brings us to a still place of peacefulness in the middle of life's adversities.

Karl Paulnack, Director of Music at Boston Conservatory in his address to the freshman class at Boston Conservatory conveys the power of music to bring the human spirit to a place of peace in the middle of a chaotic world. In encouraging the new freshman he says,

> *One of the most profound musical compositions of all time is the Quartet for the End of Time written by French composer Olivier Messier in 1940. Messier was 31 years old when France entered the war against Nazi Germany. He was captured by the Germans in June of 1940, sent across Germany in a cattle car and imprisoned in a concentration camp.*
>
> *He was fortunate to find a sympathetic prison guard who gave him paper and a place to compose. There were three other musicians in the camp, a cellist, a violinist, and a clarinetist, and Messier wrote his quartet with these specific plays in mind. It was performed in January 1941 for four thousand prisoners and guards in the prison camp. Today it is one of the most famous masterworks in the repertoire.*
>
> *Given what we have since learned about life in the concentration camps, why would anyone in his right mind waste time and energy writing or playing music Why? Well, in a place where people are only focused on survival, on the bare necessities, the obvious conclusion is that art must be, somehow, essential for life Art is part of survival; art is part of the human spirit, an unquenchable expression of who we are. Art is one of the ways in which we say, "I am alive, and my life has meaning".*
>
> *Well, my friends, someday at 8PM someone is going to walk into your concert hall and bring you a mind that is confused, a heart that is overwhelmed, a soul that is weary. Whether they go out whole again will depend partly on how well you do your craft.*

Music brings us to the place where we can be well, and **Still, *in One Peace***. In the simple space of an octave , in the limitless variations of rhythms, the peace and hope music can provide will never be exhausted.

There is much music in the air.

Music all around

The world is full of music. Take as much as you require.

It will help you cope with anything.

This music, music ever divine.

Be still, in music. Be alive in its joy and beauty. At rest in its peace. And if you think that can't happen in the small space of your world upon this earth, think then of the possibilities that can be found in the small space of an octave.

Resource: MoviePhone Plots/Internet/My Life in Ruins

Chapter Thirteen

A Look at Nature –
Beauty Perceived with the Serene Mind

Love all that has been created by God, both the whole and every grain of sand. Love every leaf, and every ray of light. Love the beasts and the birds, love the plants, love every separate fragment. If you love each separate fragment, you will understand the mystery of the whole resting in God.
Fyodor Dostoyevsky

The tree that moves some to tears of joy is in the eyes of others only a green thing that stands in the way.
Henry David Thoreau

You cannot perceive beauty but with the serene mind.
Henry David Thoreau

Go to a place, a still place, live deliberately there – to front only the essential facts of life and learn what it has to teach. This is living.
Henry David Thoreau

The morning glory which blooms for an hour differs not at heart from the giant pine – which lives for a thousand years.
Zen Poem

I walk on the shore among thousands of shells washed up on the beach. Selecting a few as summer keepsakes I am aware my fingers have chosen sea shells no other eye has seen. From the vast assortment, I have salvaged a few "separate fragments" of the beauty that is spread along the coastline. Observing their color and shape, I realize I "love all that has been created by God, both the "whole" of the thousands of varieties tossed among the surf, and every shell, like every speck of sand."

My eyes take in the vast coastline of sand as the waves crash along the beach. I bend down, take a handful of sand, letting each fleck sift through my fingers. Once again I affirm "I love all that has been created by God, both the whole of the sand stretched out before my eyes, as far as I can see, and every grain of sand, that my eyes perceive in microscopic detail." Looking intently at each granule, I become intimate with the sand. To love each separate fragment of the sand, I understand the mystery of the whole resting in God.

When you walk in the woods and take the time to lift a fallen tree trunk and observe a world of ants, slugs, snails or centipedes, most likely they will live out their lifespan with only your eye observing their world of mulch and moss. When you observe them beneath rocks or logs, you realize that you are one with every fragment, every insect, every bug, and gently return the rock, log and tree trunk to their undisturbed dwelling in a forest world of insects. You realize the deep contentment and inner peace that comes from loving all that has been created by God. You are careful not to step on ants.

When I lie under a tree, spending intimate moments with the meadow, the tree becomes more than a cool shelter on a torrid summer day. I see a deeper meaning in the tree. Toyahiko Kagawa said, "In times of quietness our hearts should be like trees lifting their branches to the sky to draw down strength which they will need to face the storms that will surely come."

As I look at each leaf, each separate fragment of the tree, I understand the mystery of the whole of resting in God. I understand what it means to be like a tree. They remind me of the strength I search for in facing storms that will surely come into my life.

Watch a leaf gently fall from a branch in an autumn wood, making a carpet on the ground in preparation for the winter frost that brings with it swirling snowflakes that no other eye will ever see in their quiet descent to hush the forest's sounds. When you do, you are a part of every fragment, every leaf, every snowflake held in nature's silence and peace, as you stand in the mysterious resting of the wholeness of God.

When I recline in a field, and place my eyes close to the blades of grass, looking so intently that I can see each blade entering the soil, I become intimate with the grass. I understand that we are "all like grass that withers and blows away."

When I watch whales on the coastline of Cape Cod, Massachusetts, I fall in love with the mammals. Watching dolphins swim and break the surface of the ocean in evening twilight, as a sailboat drifts quietly on the horizon, I touch the mystery of the whole of resting in God's natural beauty and creation painted on the landscapes of my world. I find myself in the still peace, in the mystery of the whole resting in God that brings purpose, beauty, meaning and inspiration to my spirit.

Each dawn, birds begin their chorus to welcome me to the mystery of the whole resting in God. The throttled song becomes a Sabbath morning assurance, that life is new and good. That all things dead find new meaning and purpose. I am reminded of sparrows that need not fear when they fall because they know something of the mystery of the whole resting in God, a God who is there for them when they fall. A night-time of despair and fear can dissipate with the sound of a simple chirp, repeated like a mantra of assurance that with daybreak comes the light of new possibilities and beginnings.

I love the plants, the forest flowers, the meadow blossoms, the Queen Anne's Lace, even the yellow dandelion. "The morning glory which blooms for an hour differs not at heart from the giant pine – which lives for a thousand years." I love every separate fragment. I find myself understanding the mystery of the whole resting in God. To stand by a giant Redwood, or to hold the tiny bud of a flower, I realize that they do not differ from each other. I do not differ from them.

Everything is transformed. I am transformed. I am no more, nor no less than the leaf, the beast, the bird, the light, the plant, the shell, the grain of sand, the whale, the dolphin. Everything takes upon itself a purpose in its presence for my eye to see. The tree that I recline under on my front lawn is 'the tree that moves some to tears of joy, while in the eyes of others it is only a green thing that stands in the way."

Henry David Thoreau says, "You cannot perceive beauty but with the serene mind." When we allow our minds to be still, in the peace that all of creation provides for our wholeness and well-being, we understand the mysteries of the interconnectedness of our lives with every separate fragment. As we love every separate fragment, we understand the mystery of the interconnectedness of the whole resting in God's creation. We must "go to a place, a still place, live deliberately there – to front only the essential facts of life and learn what it has to teach. This is living."

To go to a still place, living deliberately there, is something each of us must do in order to allow our lives to be *Still, in One Peace*. We realize that life is not made up of separate fragments, each thing, creature, leaf, beast, bird, person separated from each other. We are all the mystery of the whole resting in God. Since we are all held within the mystery of the whole resting in God, and if we are to love every separate fragment, then we will have to take seriously the times we leave these separate fragments harmed, neglected, broken to pieces out of carelessness and recklessness, bringing harm to our environment, to one another and even to ourselves. We bring blight upon the hearts of humankind and on the shorelines of our lands, the vastness of our skies, and upon the depth of our seas. We must think of what we do to one another and to each tiny fragment, when we observe the silky wings of monarch butterflies, or the darting flight of illusive hummingbirds, or the tear-filled eyes of frightened children when troops burst through the doors of their homes in search of terrorists and rebels.

Cup a salamander in your hands from the edge of a lake and realize that the salamander you trap in your palm is no different from the person standing on the precipice of life who would not want anyone to snap them up in clutches of oppression and injustice. Chase after the illusive fireflies that dance silently in the darkness, and realize that you would be riddled with fear if someone came unexpectedly capturing you in jars, imprisoning you in their attitudes of prejudice, hatred or resentment. Stand at the dunes in Provincetown, Cape Cod, Massachusetts, observing the marshes between the Atlantic Ocean and the wetlands, that are dried, when the tide is low, and that begin to fill with water, when the tide returns and think of the threat to our natural resources when oil spills send millions of gallons of sludge into our pristine landscapes and seas and when our rivers are polluted by waste and radioactive material.

Think of these things, as you realize that we must love every separate fragment, both the whole and every grain of sand, every river bank, and sea. Think of this when you observe the vast Grand Canyon or hidden tributaries along the shores of Louisiana and other Gulf States. Consider these things when you view the vast wide ocean, or when basking in the sun of some private beach cove on the Aegean Islands. We will never be able to rest comfortably, or be still in peace and the whole mystery of God, until we do so.

An elderly man named Marcus Chappe, a member of one of my former congregations, wanted me to take him to Rockland State Park in New York, to spread the cremated ashes of his wife Margaret. For nearly three hours we searched for a sacred spot to disperse her ashes. A supporter of the Audubon Society and Sierra Club, Marcus felt that this state park would be the most appropriate place for this sacred ritual. He and his wife often visited these lush woodlands. Each time we seemed to find just the right spot to scatter the ashes, he would survey the area to determine if the locations were free of pollutants or debris. When he noticed a submerged soda can, we moved on. If there was the slightest sheen of oil or silt glistening on the surface in the sunlight, we searched for another site. Any piece of paper on a pathway turned him on a dime seeking a more favorable setting. He wanted a pure sanctuary. The more we searched, the more discouraged we became. Eventually we found the right surroundings and prayerfully dispersed the ashes but not without having difficulty in finding a place unmarred by neglect. Not everyone loves or cares for each separate fragment of life. Just look at the trash at the side of the road.

I have been inspired by Rachel Carson's book *Silent Spring* written in 1962. As the founder of the Environmental Movement, Rachel Carson's compelling insights on what humankind continues to do to harm the earth heightens our awareness of the fragile earth and what we have done to contribute to the demise of our natural resources. We continue to threaten all fragments of life, from the tiniest of creatures, to ourselves. Just think of her thoughts in terms of the BP crisis in the Gulf of Mexico or the country of Hungary dealing with the spill of toxic red sludge that killed so many people as a dam broke, sending 264 million gallons of the by-product of aluminum from the sludge reservoir, flooding three local villages and polluting rivers including the Danube, all because of human error:

> The problem of water pollution by pesticides can be understood only in context, as part of the whole to which it belongs – the pollution of the total environment of mankind. The pollution entering our waterways comes from many sources: radioactive wastes from reactors, laboratories, and hospitals; fallout from nuclear explosions, domestic wastes from cities and towns, chemical wastes from factories. The chemical sprays applied to croplands and gardens, forests and fields.

For each of us, as for the robin in Michigan or the salmon in the Miramichi, this is a problem of ecology, of interrelationships, or interdependence. We poison the caddis flies in a stream and the salmon runs dwindle and die. We poison the gnats in a lake and the poison travels from link to link of the food chain and soon the birds of the lake margins become its victims. We spray our elms and the following springs are silent of robin-song, not because we sprayed the robins directly but because the poison traveled, step by step, through the now familiar elm leaf-earthworm-robin cycle.

It is very clear. We must love all that God has created. Both the whole and every grain of sand. Every leaf. Every ray of light. The beasts. The birds. The plants. Every separate fragment. If we love each fragment, we will understand the mystery of the whole resting in God.

We must find the still place, and live deliberately there, to front only the essential facts of life and learn what it has to teach. We must be *Still, in One Peace*. The world is far too fragmented, and life so threatened, that we must live deliberately – to front the essential facts of life and learn. To learn that we are to love all that God has created. The oil-soaked pelicans and the destroyed livelihoods of people along the Gulf region remind us of this. The displaced millions in the tent camps of Haiti after the Earthquake as well as the Tsunami in Japan, compel our minds to confront the essential facts of life. The atrocities and injustices to humanity convict us as well, as we stop to consider the Sarin Gas used against innocent civilians in Syria. Our fire-ravaged forests and flash flood-ruined landscapes make us aware that at any given moment our precious resources, our businesses and homes can be obliterated. When we live deliberately in this still place we will find ourselves Still, in His peace. In the whole resting of God. This is living.

Let us consider this question that Rachel Carson asks: "It is hard to explain to the children that the birds have been killed off, when they have learned in school that a Federal law protects the birds from killing or capture. 'Will they ever come back,' the children ask, and I don't have the answer. The elms are still dying and so are the birds. Is anything being done? Can anything be done? Can I do anything?"

Being in the still place of the whole resting in God requires that we ask such questions. We can find the answers that will lead us to that place, that still place of peace. Can I do anything? Let me first go to a still, quiet place and ponder these things. Listen to a bird chirp. Watch a chipmunk scurry through the forest floor. Observe a deer looking tenderly at her newborn fawn. Look at children crying from burns on their bodies in the Mid-East conflicts. We know what we must do in order for our world and humanity to survive in one piece. Be still, and you will also know what you must do to make sure our earth, home and human family can be **Still, in One Peace.**

Resource: Rachel Carson, *Silent Spring*. A Mariner Book Houghton Mifflin Company, NY 1962

Chapter Fourteen

Anne Frank

I simply can't build my hopes on a foundation of confusion, misery and death... I think peace and tranquility will return again.
Anne Frank

Rest is not some holy feeling that comes upon us in church. It is a state of calm, rising from a heart deeply and firmly established in God.
L. B. Cowman

To burn brightly our lives must first experience the flame. In other words, we cease to bless others when we cease to bleed.
Ignatius

People are like stained-glass windows. They sparkle and shine when the sun is out, but when the darkness sets in, their true beauty is revealed only if there is light from within.
Elisabeth Kubler-Ross

One must have chaos in oneself in order to give birth to a dancing star.
Friedrich Nietzsche

My heartstrings are tugged when I watch the ASPCA television commercial depicting the heartrending eyes of abused and abandoned animals. The forlorn stare of Tabitha reflects the sentiment, "Locked up her whole life." The description, "Never loved and left to die," tells the miserable tale of Nathaniel. The heart wrenching glance of Blondie's bruised heart rivets our concentration to the declaration that she has been "abandoned and dying from a broken heart."

To encourage contributions to fight this neglect, the commercial ends with the statement: "These are the faces of pain, *real pain!*" "Every life counts! The ASPCA will rescue animals from these abuses." Their expressions captured in slow motion are compelling recognitions of our brutality to animals.

The famished faces of children around the world speak of deeper maltreatment and desertion, making us comprehend that the "real faces of anguish" are not limited to felines or canines in ASPCA commercials. The real faces of agony are seen in people whose expressions tell the story of the mercilessness of life. Faces in which we notice no peace. Reflections in whose eyes we touch the reality of exploitation, neglect and terror.

Faces of pain! Real pain! In the sullen eyes of those cast off and injured. The screams of pain seen in the Pulitzer Prize photograph of the nude child walking in panic as she screams on the war torn roadsides of Vietnam. The face of pain, real pain of elderly and homeless people, derelict and forsaken in cardboard boxes on city streets. The face of AIDS or the anguish on faces of those who have lost loved ones in tragedy, disaster and acts of terrorism. The faces of pain of children burning from the use of Sarin Gas and chemical weapons in Syria. We see the pain in the forlorn look of strangers as we pass them by.

There is a face of one young girl whose life has given the world a veritable manifestation of hope, as her upbeat smile and cheerful gaze reflect a secret peace and purity that comes from a wisdom beyond her years and an innocence untainted by a capitulation to fear, hate and cynicism. It is a face of hope captured in the enduring portrait of a young Anne Frank, the teenager whose journal recorded the secret hopes of her heart while secluded in an Amsterdam, Holland, hideaway from the Nazis in war torn Europe. This visage of hope was placed on the book jacket of the Diary of Anne Frank. Her portrait commands respect, sympathy, affection, gratitude and admiration.

Why am I attracted to her face? Attracted to her diary written with a wisdom and profound discernment of life by a girl whose future is endangered, but whose strength of character is uncompromising? The words by William Butler Yeats identifies my fascination with this face, this real face of hope – of Anne Frank:

"We can make our minds so like still water that when beings gather about us, they may see their own images and so live for a moment with a clearer, perhaps even with a fiercer life because of our quiet."

I concede my uncertainties and desperation to Anne Frank. To her face. Her real face of hope. Lao Tzu said, "To the mind that is still, the whole universe surrenders."

Observing the portrait of Anne Frank, the hopefulness within her smile, my life surrenders to it. I submit to her mind that is still. To her heart that beats with optimism. To her words written with confidence allowing her to say, "Despite everything, I feel people are good at heart."

Only a life that is *Still, in One Peace* can proclaim such an affirmation. Her life was a life of hope. Real Hope! Lived in the framework of bona fide pain. Valid uncertainty. Genuine fear. Authentic doubt. Despite the atrocities occurring at this time, the annihilation of six million Jews, she was able to assert: "I simply can't build my life on a foundation of confusion, misery and death... I think peace and tranquility will come again."

The stillness in the mind of Anne Frank is magnetic. I resign my fears, miseries, and confusion to the hopefulness embodied in her being.

"I simple can't build my hopes on despair," she says. Can't build. Won't build. Refuses to build. Determined not to build. Resolves not to build. In the midst of terror, the pinnacle of fear, the occurrence of confusion, the mayhem of misery, the certainty of death, the enormity of despair, her face emanates hope. Real hope! She is building, shaping, ordering, visualizing, contemplating, dreaming about hope. Peace and tranquility are manifested in the mere hoping for it.

In knowing that peace and tranquility will return again, in merely contemplating it, she makes a foregone conclusion that peace and tranquility already are a reality for her. While confined to a secret hiding place, Anne Frank knew that her anticipation of a return of peace and tranquility would not manifest itself mysteriously through the walls of her hideaway, inexplicably visualized and penetrating her self-imposed safe haven. Anne Frank had peace and tranquility within the confines of her mind.

With peace and tranquility residing in her mind, we discern that Anne Frank was able to utilize confusion, misery and thoughts of death to her advantage. Refusing to build her hope on a foundation of confusion, misery and death she acknowledged that these chaotic things are swirling around her. Her clandestine dwelling is proof that she and her family were determined to survive as long as possible. Survive the confusion, outlast the misery, overcome the death that confronted six million people outside their walls.

Refusing to internalize the confusion, misery and death, she utilizes the chaos to nurture her hopefulness. She builds her perception on peace and tranquility.

Friedrich Nietzsche said, "One must have chaos in oneself in order to give birth to a dancing star." Anne refused to fall victim to that chaos in her confinement. Living in peace and tranquility she became a face of hope, real hope. In her smile that still radiates from the publications of her diary, we see the human spirit that can give birth to a dancing star.

Imagine if Anne Frank locked herself in solitary confinement with her cell mates being terror, confusion, misery and death. It would simply have amounted to being buried alive. Her face radiated hope. Real hope. Hope endures all things. Believes all things. Believes and imagines that peace and tranquility will return again. To be able to write this declaration is to have imagined that peace and tranquility exists despite evidence to the contrary.

Carl Sagan, the scientist said, "Imagination will often carry us to worlds that never were. But without it, we go nowhere." In the imprisonment of her apartment dwelling, Anne Frank's imagination continued to take her to worlds that never were – a world she would not design or build on a foundation of confusion or misery. Her imagination was her sanity. It gave to her three-room world a boundless world of hopefulness. Without that imagination, or her spirit that resided in the stillness of one peace, we would never have come to know the name Anne Frank, or the portrait that evokes such peace, tranquility and hope.

Elisabeth Kubler-Ross who wrote about the experience of death and dying said, "People are like stained-glass windows. They sparkle and shine when the sun is out, but when the darkness sets in their true beauty is revealed only if there is light from within."

Anne Frank was one of those human beings whose true beauty, simple love, profound wisdom and contagious hope, shone from within her during one of history's darkest moments. Ignatius said, "To burn brightly, our lives must first experience the flame. In other words we cease to bless others when we cease to bleed."

Make no mistake about it. Anne Frank and her family knew the intensity of the flames. Many of the Jews were burned by those flames in concentration camps. Her memoir and journal has been a blessing to the world because their hearts and souls knew what it meant to bleed. Yet, they would not submit to the reality of building their lives on a foundation of confusion, misery and death.

Anne Frank knew one truth: "peace and tranquility would someday return." She knew this through the bleeding efforts, her legacy in writing. Her blessing today is a result of her bleeding refusing to succumb to hopelessness.

I look at her sweet portrait. Her face beams brightly with hope. Real hope! It is a face of a young Jewish girl who has taught me how to be *Still, in One Peace.*

There is a peaceful rest in her portrait. "Rest is not some holy feeling that comes upon us in church. It is a state of calm, rising from a heart deeply and firmly established in God." Her rest came not to her in a synagogue or "church" – it came to her in her abandonment and hideaway. She is a portrait, a *Still-life,* in One peace.

Only such a heart that Anne Frank possessed could build life on a foundation of hope and know that despite the chaos, death, and misery around her, she could be *Still, in One Peace.* The chaos within her gave birth to a dancing star. Stars named hope and tranquility. In her we see that truth, love and hope abide in every circumstance.

I want to take Anne Frank into my arms and heart and dance with hope, in the promise of peace and tranquility, that comes from a mind that is *Still, in One Peace.* When I do, I let her hold my fears and confusion. I let her lead, as just seeing her young portrait, I am reminded to build my life on a foundation of peace and tranquility that can be found in no other place than in the stillness of that One peace. Anne Frank and her family were eventually discovered and imprisoned. She died in the concentration camps shortly before Europe was liberated. But ah, her face reminds me, that even at the end, she was *Still, in One Peace*, still building her life on peace and tranquility. Out of all that chaos, I believe she is a "star" dancing among stars, in the stillness of One peace.

Chapter Fifteen

With God in Your Heart Nothing is Lacking – All Things Fade Away

Let nothing disturb you, nothing distress you
While all things fade away
God is unchanging
Be patient for with God in your heart
Nothing is lacking
God is enough
Julian of Norwich

Where there is faith, there is love
where there is love, there is peace
where there is peace, there is God
and where there is God there is no need.
Leo Tolstoy

I remember the disturbing, distressing feeling when my parents dropped me off at West Virginia Wesleyan College for my freshman year in 1966. After spending two days helping me settle into dorm life, sharing a room for the first time with an absolute stranger, and attending various student orientation programs, we said our goodbyes, with tenacious hugs and kisses. I stood at the curbside, watching the red tail lights of their car fade in the distance as they left Buckhannon, West Virginia, traveling the winding roads of the Upshur County mountains that would return them to their New Jersey home – without me! I was 18, stranded on campus, excited and scared to death.

My parents faded into their world without me. It was a difficult, painful, disturbing and distressing transition. Aside from several summer camp experiences, this was my first major separation from what had formed my world up to this point.

It was also a difficult transition because of the sudden death of my grandfather just a few months before. Though embarking on a new adventure, the separation from family was distressing. His death devastated me.

While I can still envision those fading tail lights of my parents' car and the feeling of the trauma that image created, my Dad died from Alzheimer's in August, 2012. Mom turns 90 this November, confronting me with a reality check that our time together on earth is quickly fading away. This thought disturbs and distresses me. It is literally a heartbreaking thought. It will not be too long before I begin living life without either of them. Without their physical presence, that is.

Another reality check is the fact that I am 65 years old. It has been said that when the "physical eyesight begins to diminish, the spiritual eyesight begins to increase." Since I am of the nature not to merely view life through my physical eyes, my spiritual insight, as it deepens and broadens, reminds me that, if I look at life only through my physical eyes, I will put myself on the delusional trip that I'm still in my mid 30s, enjoying life without any regard to the spiritual insights that can shape one's maturing years, to discern, that, while I might only have a diminished amount of years to live, the best of life and living is still ahead.

When we live through the spiritual eyesight that reveals the true essence and meaning of living and our purpose in life, the best years of life are always ahead, always now, no matter our age or limitations. If I live only by my physical eyesight, than I will continue to be distressed and disturbed when I stand in front of the mirror and see my sagging pecks, shake my loose triceps and biceps, observe my expanding waistline and jiggle the stretched skin under my chin. Living only by that physical eyesight, I'll frantically run to the gym in an attempt to delay the inevitable, rather than exercising as a routine to keep my body in shape for the sole purpose of knowing that attention to the physical aspects of my diminishing abilities, will continue to strengthen my spirit and soul, as I treat my body well as long as I am physically able.

As we begin to confront things and people that pass away, fade away, we begin to look at life more with spiritual insight, a vision that begins to open our eyes to what is most meaningful in life and precious to our hearts. It is unfortunate that some people, who when their physical eyesight begins to diminish, are unable to permit the sense of a spiritual insight to enrich their moments with abiding assurance, quiet reflection and inner solitude and comfort. They continue with diminished physical eyesight, searching for the things, out there, that only bring temporary comfort and security at best, as they live their days in the dim unknown of life that is fading away. Such days are distressing and disturbing, if we look at life only through our physical eyes. When we do, we wind up trusting in things that fade away and eventually provide us with nothing to sustain us.

All things fade away! The limelight fades away. Looks fade. Flowers wither and fade. So does grass. Time fades. Years fade away. The sun fades away. Eyesight fades. Dreams fade. People move away and fade away from our memory. Memory fades. Agility fades. Our muscle tone fades. Supple skin fades. Learning fades. Taste buds fade. Sense of smell fades. Motivation fades. Libido fades. Love fades. Marriages fade. Relationships fade. Julian of Norwich was right – *all things* fade away!

If all things fade away, our spiritual sight and insight must bring us to one conclusion: while all things fade away, the source of peace is unchanging. That source is unchanging. That source is enough. Nothing is lacking. While all things fade away, God is unchanging. Such spiritual insight and eyesight will bring us to that place where we can be still in the confidence that while all things fade away, nothing will ever be lacking, for God is enough.

When we can look at life and our lives through such spiritual eyesight, we can affirm that with such faith, there is love. Where there is that love, there is peace. Where there is peace, there is God. Where we can be still in God, in that One peace, there is no need. While all things fade away in the end, God is enough. Where there is God, there is no need. No need to fret and worry when things fade away. Nothing is lacking. God is enough.

In our summer cottage there are two treasured pictures of my family on the beach. Mom is helping my sister who is five and me a toddler, dig holes in the sand. The other picture has my Dad lifting me in his arms and my sister playing at his side. These are images of happy days on the beach.

At the end of one of our summers at the shore, my parents were struggling to keep their legs steady as they walked along the uneven sand to the ramp that led to the boardwalk. My cousin Althea urged me to capture this daily familiar image with a photograph of Mom and Dad walking with their canes, hobbling up the ramp, in their slow steady, yet fading pace. The contrast of the two pictures on our cottage wall, of summers past and the image of our present days on the beach, are etched in my mind. I watch them walk in the distance, imagining them as those red tail lights fading in the distance as they left my college town. For a moment this image is disturbing and distressing. But then my spiritual eyes kick in and I have a different vision. While all things fade away, nothing is lacking. God is enough. I look at my parents, at life and say to myself, where there is faith, there is love and where there is love there is peace. Where there is peace, there is God. Suddenly the spiritual wisdom overrides the distressing and disturbing thoughts. Where there is God, there is no need. I find myself having everything. Nothing is ever lacking when I am Still, in God's peace. God's peace lasts forever. It never fades away.

I watch them and a happiness washes over me like the waves that I hear from the surf.

Love never fades away. When there is love, there is peace. When there is peace, there is God. When there is God, there is no need. For we have all the love that we need. We find the fullness of that life, when our spiritual eyesight reveals that we are certain of the peace that comes from being *Still, in One Peace*. All things fade away. But there is one thing that I am forever certain of – I feel the peace that comes from resting in God's love, while everything else fades away. In that stillness, nothing is lacking. There is no need. Find this truth by looking at life through your spiritual eyes. God's love never ends or disappears like red tail lights on a winding West Virginia roadway to leave us standing alone. God's love never ends when we are standing at the grave of a loved one whom we will see no more. God's love will never fade away.

Chapter Sixteen

Wrestling With Our Demons

Confront the dark parts of yourself, and work to banish them with illumination and forgiveness. Your willingness to wrestle with your demons will cause your angels to sing. Use the past as fuel, as a reminder of your strength.
August Wilson (Author of the play, *Fences*)

Our souls are restless, till they find their rest in Thee.
St. Augustine

Appearing in the dark window
Is a phantom face,
wrestling with demons
in the dark places of my life,
as the train speeds down the track
swallowing me into a tunnel of greater obscurity.
My eyes are trapped in glass,
encasing my spirit, as they
stare,
wonder,
and search
for the person hiding behind those anxious eyes
an apparition of deficiency
a tenuous spirit
whose shattered heart,
discarded dreams,
are dumped between tracks and backyard fences
overgrown, unattended
Mingled among trash and
rusted supermarket carts and

Piles of tarred railroad ties
gnarled by brush and twisted vines
choking me with their heaped up lies.
Reflections in the window
speeding with villain velocity down the track
Heading nowhere
Debating if I'd want the chance to start over, back.
In the nocturnal uncertainty
I confront my demons
in the eyes that stare into my world
I know the stranger's eyes,
We are night time bedfellows,
but I don't know who really stares at me
or where I'm headed
(though I know where I've been)
Feeling caught between winding tracks and backyard fences
and twisted trees
and misshapen fantasies
In the window of a nearby seat
another likeness appears, of
a stranger, eyes taut in sleep
I speculate what lies behind the masquerade of his dark reflection
does he know his destination
or the demons that lurk behind the darkness of his eyes?
"Mind the gap, when you get off the train," the conductor says.
Wide disparity of darkness and light
lie before my feet, around each curve, as I travel
the corridor behind backyard fences
where I rarely confront those phantom faces,
except between tracks and backyard fences
where demons lurk.
I peer at the stranger's eyes in the window reflection
of the seat ahead of me
and speculate

if he knows what demons lurk around the twists ahead.
Or prowl within.
The cavernous eyes of my phantom stranger
remind me
there are demons to confront
around the bend.
Within.
Will they betray me
Or can I banish them?

I wrote these words to remind me that there are always shadows within me in need of illumination and forgiveness.

Sometimes we banish our demons by simply ignoring them! Pretending they don't exist.

But they are always lurking within. We all have them. Like Abraham Lincoln said in his Inaugural Speech, we would much rather appeal to the "better angels of our nature." We avoid dealing with the shadowy places of our lives. We say, "Hey, I'm a pretty good person, at heart!" If that's the case, why are those hearts so restless?

Part of me wants to share only the better aspects of the angels of our nature rather than consider the reality that there is much darkness within each of us, a darkness that causes us much unrest. We cannot move into the center of peace, into the stillness of peace, until we deal with the phantom shadows in our lives. Until we do, our hearts will be restless. This book will have served no purpose, unless we deal with the issues of our shadows.

We can be touched by the better angels of our nature, while simultaneously confronting the dark parts of our selves. August Wilson said, "Your willingness to wrestle with your demons will cause your angels to sing." Angels and Demons co-exist. To confront those dark parts of our lives, will cause the angels not only to sing. It will cause them to bring harmony to the Still, centered place of our lives. Their voices will banish those demons. We must confront the dark parts of ourselves. I remind myself of this when speeding down those dark corridors on a train between the tracks and backyard fences. We must have a "willingness" and not a resistance to dealing with our demons.

If we are going to change we must confront these dark places with illumination and forgiveness. In doing so, we are asking light and grace to provide a sacred place where we can be healed and a hopeful place where we come to find that we are forgiven. Just look back at the times you have known this to be true and you will discover that August Wilson is correct that in the remembrance of those times you will be "reminded of your strength" that allowed you to confront the dark parts of yourself, and survive and overcome them. Even banish them.

Who wants to deal with demons? None of us do!

Recently appearing in the theater section of the newspaper was an ad for the movie *Paranormal Activity*. The ad claimed the movie to be "one of the scariest movies of all time. You will be affected as it's hard to ignore the imprint it leaves on your psyche. Nightmares are guaranteed. Bloody disgusting." I often wonder why people choose to see a movie that fills their psyche with nightmares and horror, movies like Freddie Krueger, Halloween, Nightmare on Elm Street, Chainsaw Massacre and the newly released, "Take My Soul." We'll sit in a dark theater, biting our nails, jumping scared to death in our seats at some horrible, ghoulish unexpected scene, closing our eyes in fear. Yet, we spend little time, confronting the shadows of our own lives. We just don't want to deal with inner demons.

"In contemporary Western Occultist tradition a demon, such as Choronzon, the "Demon of the Abyss" is a useful metaphor for certain inner psychological processes, known as inner demons. Usually, when we think of demons we think of them in terms of the evil supernatural person, a devil, a persistently tormenting person, force or passion within our lives. The demon of drug addiction. The demon of the bottle. We will also think of it in terms of sexuality, when we coyly refer to someone as, "you little devil, you!!" (Demons, Wikipedia)

There are, however, interesting origins of the word, aside from *daimon*, spirit or divine power. *Kakadaimonia* in the Greek derivation of the word means, "misfortune." Misfortune manifests itself within us that can cause us to maintain spiteful natures and confining us to living lives of regret.

There is another derivation which I find interesting found in the word *daiesthai*, which means to "divide, distribute." The word does not have the connotation of evil or malevolence. It simply means to "divide" or "distribute," pulled in all directions, distracted from unity of mind, purpose and being." A restless heart that is divided. A will that is not rooted in purpose. In the Old Testament Book of Job, there is a conversation between the Devil and God. God asks the Devil where he is from. He replies, "I'm from here and there, to and fro." "Like a wind that blows where it will." Divided from the peace and wholeness that God provides.

We all have our personal cheering section!!!! They are not merely people who are our advocates, mentors, family. Your willingness to wrestle with your demons will cause your angels to sing. They sing within you! When you work hard to confront and banish those dark parts of yourself, with illumination and forgiveness, they raise their voices. That kind of love and light within you can cast out the darkness, the demons and the divisiveness.

Let your darkness work hard for you, as you work hard dealing with your darkness.

In his book *Shadows*, D. H. Lawrence said, "And if tonight my soul may find her peace in sleep and sink in good oblivion, and in the morning wake like a new opened flower, then I have been dipped again in God and new – created." (1932). And if *tonight* we can find any sense of peace, it will come from being Still, in the One Peace of God. As your life is moving down the track, between backyard fences where the demons lurk around every bend, find rest in the Still, One Peace of God and find your life "new – created." When you confront the dark places of your life, you will not only find angels singing for you, you will find the illumination of life, hope and peace, right in the center of your darkness.

Antoine de Saint-Exupery said, "Night, when words fade and things come alive – when the destructive analysis of day is done, and all that is truly important becomes whole and sound again. When man reassembles his fragmentary self and grows with the calm of a tree." The dark, restful peace of night is the time when we can cease doing the destructive analysis of day, well into night, we discover all that is truly important. Like being *Still, in One Peace*, the place where we become whole and sound again. We spend so much time looking at the imperfections staring at us through the phantom reflections in the window as we travel the tracks of our lives behind the backyard fences. We all have demons and shadows, our prejudices, fears and worries. Our phantom faces tell us that we are imperfect.

But look at the darkness of the word "imperfect" through a different light. IM Perfect. In Me, the PERFECT peace of God dwells, if we let the illumination and the forgiveness reassemble our fragmentary self, with all its fears and imperfections, into the Stillness of One Peace. The angels will sing and cheer us on. The better angels of our natures will sing as well. Remember, in that Still Peace, you will be stronger than you think! The illuminating light and peace of God is already within you, before any darkness or demon comes in. Knowing this will keep you *Still, in One Peace*. Still, in God's grace.

Resource: Demons, Wikipedia.

Chapter Seventeen

Gossip

There is so much good in the worst of us and so much bad in the best of us that it ill behaves any of us to find fault with the rest of us.
James Truslow Adams

For every kind of beasts, and of birds, and of serpents, and of things in the sea, is tamed, and hath been tamed of mankind: But the tongue can no man tame; it is an unruly evil, full of deadly poison.
James (ch. III, v. 7-8)

A wound made by an arrow will cicatrize and heal; a forest felled by the axe will spring up again in new growth; but a wound made by the tongue will never heal.
Mahabharata

A wound from a tongue is worse than a wound from the sword; the latter affects only the body – the former, the spirit, the soul.
Pythagoras

Gossip is always a personal confession either of malice or imbecility, and the young should not only shun it, but by the most thorough culture relieve themselves from all temptation to indulge in it. It is a low, frivolous, and too often a dirty business. There are country neighborhoods in which it rages like a pest. Churches are split in pieces by it. Neighbors are made enemies by it for life. In many persons it degenerates into a chronic disease, which is practically incurable. Let the young cure it while they may.
Josiah Gilbert Holland

It is only before those who are glad to hear it, and anxious to spread it, that we find it easy to speak ill of others.
Jean Antoine Petit-Senn

At thirteen I learned my first lesson about gossip.

During my elementary school years at Madison Avenue Elementary School, in Newark, New Jersey, my parents participated in the Parent Teachers Association, performing in the annual talent show to help raise funds for school projects. One year they portrayed Elisa Doolittle and Professor Higgins, performing *All I Want is a Room Somewhere*, from *My Fair Lady* and *Side By Side*, the 1927 Harry Woods classic, singing, "Oh we ain't got a barrel of money, maybe we're ragged and funny, but we'll travel along, singin our song, side by side."

Mom didn't think the director was particularly apt at running a stage show. She made the critical assessment during dinner one evening around the kitchen table. The following day, while hanging out in the school playground before the bell called classes into session, I was talking with my classmate, John Williams, who happened to be the son of the director of the variety show. I told him my mother thought his mother lacked the skills to direct a musical revue. "My Mom thinks your Mom doesn't know what she's doing," I said!!!

At the next cast rehearsal Mom was puzzled by the cold reception received from the director. At a subsequent practice the frosty rebuff persisted. Mom heard from another parent in the cast that the director was furious at Mom's criticism. It didn't take Mom long to wade through her embarrassment, tracing the origin of the gossip back to the evening meal and my eavesdropping on the conversation between my parents. I received a lashing the likes of which would have, today resulted in a visit from DYFS, the child protection and welfare agency. This confrontation enlightened me to the harm caused by "gossiping," to the ramifications of parental anger, and to the wisdom that comes from keeping my mouth shut in the future.

A few years later I saw the 1961 drama film, *The Children's Hour*, based on the 1934 play by Lillian Hillman. That movie revealed a more hazardous capability of gossip. I was traumatized by its portrayal of the detriment of gossip.

The movie starred Audrey Hepburn, Shirley MacLaine and James Garner. In the United Kingdom the movie was given the title, *The Loudest Whisper*. Today, I think of this tragedy when I consider the destruction gossip instigates.

Former College classmates Martha Dobie played by Shirley MacLaine and Karen Wright played by Audrey Hephurn, open a private school for girls in provincial New England. Joe Cardin, who is played by James Garner, finally wins the affection of Karen, who, after several rejections, agrees to marry him. Joe is related to wealthy Amelia Tilford, whose granddaughter Mary is a student at the private school. Mary is a spoiled, devious child. When Mary is caught in a lie involving another student, Karen punishes her by refusing to allow her to attend the boat races to be held that weekend. Infuriated, Mary retaliates by inventing a story about Martha and Karen being involved in a lesbian relationship, securing the corroboration of another student through blackmail, over a piece of jewelry she has stolen.

Mary tells her grandmother that she caught the two teachers kissing. A distraught Mrs. Tilford reveals the sordid details to the other parents, who subsequently remove their daughters from the school. The teachers' reputations are destroyed.

Joe confronts Karen, asking her if the rumor is true. His mistrust is evident. The wedding is called off.

When Martha learns about the breakup, she confesses to Karen that she always had feelings for her, but never acted on them.

The grandmother eventually learns the story is a fabrication and visits the teachers, offering an apology and promising restitution, which Karen cannot accept. By this point, the damage is irreparable.

Martha and Karen talk about their future. As the conversation intensifies, Karen decides to take a walk, needing space to think. In her absence, a desperate Martha hangs herself, leaving Karen at her gravesite, as Joe Cardin watches her walk away in the movie's closing scene. (MoviePhone Plots/Internet/Children's Hour)

Gossip destroys lives. It is a terminal malignancy in any relationship or situation. Its harm is devastating. The Old Testament book of Proverbs 25:18 says, "Telling lies about someone is as harmful as hitting him with an axe, or wounding him with a sword, or shooting him with a sharp arrow." Leviticus 19:16 says, "Do not go about spreading slander among your people." The commandments are also very clear, "Do not bear false witness against thy neighbor."

Recently, a dear friend and colleague called to inform me that his 40-year marriage was being terminated. He wanted to tell me before I heard about it through the gossip mill. He was not at an emotional point to share details. I didn't need to know them either. He needed to talk through his pain and remorse. He desired understanding and compassion from a non-threatening, non-judgmental friend.

I knew the depth of his trauma from the demise of my own marriage. I recalled the times people said to me, regarding my divorce, "How are you going to handle *that* scandal?" The mere use of the word *scandal,* made me realize my life was already being chewed up and devoured in the rumor gossip mill. I've continued to adopt the position that James Truslow Adams expressed in his view on the subject of gossip: "There is so much good in the worst of us and so much bad in the best of us that it ill behoves any of us to find fault with the rest of us." We would think twice about gossip if we took James Adams' wisdom to heart.

Unfortunately, many people revel in gossiping, like the Jane Austen character who thrives on it: "For what do we live, but to make sport of our neighbors and laugh at them in our turn?"

The Pillow Sermon from the movie *Doubt* provides the most articulate description of the power of gossip that I have ever heard. The visual image of "gossip" portrayed in the cinema portrayal of the 2005 Pulitzer Prize winner for drama, written by John Patrick Shanley, clearly demonstrates the futility of attempting to retrieve slander and gossip once it is released from the unbridled mouth.

Sister Aloysius Beauvier, played by Meryl Streep, principal of St. Nicholas Catholic School in the Bronx, New York, is suspicious about the possible sexual misconduct of her parish priest, Father Brendon Flynn, played by Philip Seymour Hoffman. The time is 1964, long before the explosive issues surrounding pedophilia become a major news item in the Catholic Church.

The winds of change are sweeping through this tight-knit religious community, and charismatic priest Father Flynn is doing his best to adapt by revisiting the school's notoriously strict disciplinary practices. Unfortunately Father Flynn's progressive ideas stand in stark contrast to the longstanding beliefs of Sister Aloysius Beauvier, the iron-willed principal, who believes that an oppressive environment of punishment and fear is the only way to keep the student body in line. Suddenly into this tempestuous environment appears young Donald Miller, St. Nicholas' first black student. When hopeful innocent Sister James (played by Amy Adams) reluctantly reveals to Sister Beauvier that Father Flynn and Donald have been spending an unusual amount of time together in the church rectory, the unrelentingly righteous headmistress begins a merciless crusade to reveal the beloved clergyman as a lecherous child molester and have him permanently expunged from the school. Yet despite her moral certainty that Father Flynn has committed such an unspeakable transgression, Sister Beauvier has not a shred of actual evidence to back up her audacious claim. Now, as Sister Beauvier and

Father Flynn enter into an epic battle of wills, the shock waves set into motion by their explosive confrontation threaten to destroy one man's reputation and tear apart the entire surrounding community. (Moviephone Plots, Internet)

John Patirck Shanley, includes the pillow sermon in his script, a sermon that Father Flynn delivers to his Bronx congregation to drive home his point about gossip:

A woman was gossiping with a friend about a man she hardly knew – I know none of you have ever done this – that night she had a dream. A great hand appeared over her and pointed down at her. She was immediately seized with an overwhelming sense of guilt. The next day she went to confession. She got the old parish priest, Father O'Rourke, and she told him the whole thing.

'Is gossiping a sin?' she asked the old man. 'Was that the hand of God Almighty pointing a finger at me? Should I be asking your absolution? Father, tell me, have I done something wrong?'

(Irish Brogue)

'Yes!' Father O'Rourke answered her. 'Yes, you ignorant, badly brought up female! You have borne false witness against your neighbor, you have played fast and loose with his reputation, and you should be heartily ashamed!'

So the woman said she was sorry and asked for forgiveness.

'Not so fast!' says O'Rourke. 'I want you to go home, take a pillow up on your roof, cut it open with a knife, and return here to me!'

So the woman went home, took a pillow off her bed, a knife from the drawer, went up the fire escape to the roof, and stabbed the pillow. Then she went back to the old parish priest as instructed.

'Did you gut the pillow with the knife?' he says.

'Yes, Father.'

'And what was the result?'

'Feathers,' she said.

'Feathers?' he repeated.

'Feathers everywhere, Father!'

'Now I want you to go back and gather up every last feather that flew out on the wind!'

'Well,' she said, 'it can't be done. I don't know where they went. The wind took them all over.'

*'And that,' said Father O'Rourke, 'is **GOSSIP!**'*

In the name of the Father, the Son, and the Holy Ghost, Amen

This is the power of Gossip! Once it is released, it can't be retrieved, as the thousands of feathers floating through the air in slow motion in the movie to support Father Flynn's sermon illustrates.

It is clear. When we gossip, the one who is gossiping and the one whom the gossip is about will never be able to find themselves, still, in One peace. The tongue is a dangerous weapon. It can destroy lives. It is best to keep it "still." To refrain from gossiping. When we gossip we are not promoters of peace. We are harbingers of slander and ill will at the expensive of someone else's life and to the diminishment of our own. We simply can't find ourselves *Still, in One Peace* when we gossip.

Do you want to spread poison? Or do you want to extend peace? Your answer will determine whether you will find your heart, *Still, in One Peace.*

"It is only before those who are glad to hear it, (gossip) and anxious to spread it, that we find it easy to speak ill of others." This is a point well taken. Stay away from gossipers! If by chance, you can't distance yourself from the one who is gossiping, refrain from participating in it. You will find your life to be *Still, in One Peace*, if you do. Cure the habit while you may! Your heart will stay in peace, in still peace, because you do.

Resource: MoviePhone Plots, Internet, Doubt, Children's Hour

Chapter Eighteen

War

War does not determine who is right – only who is left.
Bertrand Russell

Mankind must put an end to war or war will put an end to mankind.
J. F. Kennedy

For my enemy is dead, a man divine as myself is dead, I look where he lies white-faced and still in the coffin – I draw near, Bend down and touch lightly with my lips the white face in the coffin.
Walt Whitman, "Reconciliation" used in Ralph Vaughan Williams' Dona Nobis Pacem (Grant us peace)

Man is the only animal that deals in that atrocity of atrocities, War. He is the only one that gathers his brethren about him and goes forth in cold blood and calm pulse to exterminate his kind. He is the only animal that for sordid wages will march out and help to slaughter strangers of his own species who have done him no harm and with whom he has no quarrel... And in the intervals between campaigns he washes the blood off his hands and works for "the universal brotherhood of man" – with his mouth.
Mark Twain

Christian P. Engeldrum.

The name has been on my refrigerator since November 29, 2004.

Christian P. Engeldrum.

His face has been in my mind since November 29, 2004.

Christian P. Engeldrum.

His body has disturbed my conscience since November 29, 2004.

Christian P. Engledrum. Born November 19, 1965. Died November 29, 2004. A solider in the American Armed Forces. One of the first casualties of the Iraq war. I stand before his casket, looking at his "still" body. Broken. Lying there, still, in one piece. His life sacrificed, so that we might live. Live in freedom. That we might reside, Still, in peace. I look at his flag-draped coffin, his body shrouded in uniform, his beret adorning his forehead, a halo of peace. My silent thoughts thank him for his sacrifice. Tears well up in my eyes with appreciation. Tears fill my heart with gratitude. Tears tug at my conscience with anger that Christian P. Engeldrum had to be deployed to Iraq. Anger that at 39 he had to lose his life. Leave a wife and family. As I look at his still repose, I ponder the thought, "war does not determine who is right – only who is left."

Josef Stalin said, "The death of one man is tragedy. The death of millions is a statistic."

I look at Christian Engeldrum and pray that he not be a mere statistic of this war. Standing before him alone, I am reminded that his death, this one death, is undeniably a tragedy, giving credence to Plato's words, "It is only the dead who have seen the end of war." Mother Teresa speaks to my heart as I stand before Christian Engeldrum's body, remembering her words: "If we have no peace it is because we have forgotten that we belong to each other."

"War may sometimes be a necessary evil. But no matter how necessary, it is always an evil, never a good. We will not learn how to live together in peace by killing each other's children." These words from President Jimmy Carter confirm that Christian Engeldrum is a tragedy of the necessary evil. He is also a sacrifice for our freedom. War killed Christian Engeldrum. Someone's child. Someone's husband. Someone's father. I stand before his body, imagining what he might feel if the President of the United

States were standing before this open coffin. Before the body of a soldier, who lies still, in repose, in one piece, broken by the carnage of war.

Through war, some nation wins a fragile peace. Through war, it is peace itself that is broken, shattered, leaving humankind in pieces, in a temporary peace until the next engagement of nation against nation erupts upon our fragile planet that forever spins in conflict. Syria reminds us of a world continually engaged in conflict.

I've listened many times to Ralph Vaughan Williams' *Dona Nobis Pacem* since standing before the body of Christian Engledrum and as I continue to hear the growing statistics of those lost in war. The text, *Grant us Peace*, uses Walt Whitman's poems and words from the Mass, allowing Vaughan Williams to capture the horror and futility of war that leaves humankind in broken pieces. This work, along with Karl Jenkins', *The Armed Man: A Mass for Peace,* are two profound musical compositions that speak of the repulsion of war as well as the noble sacrifice of those who fight in the pursuit of peace.

Whitman's prose, *Beat! Beat! Drums* provides the text that Williams uses to describe the drums and bugles of war bursting through doors and windows, disrupting the peaceful lives of church congregations, scholars, bridal couples, and other civilians. War, a ruthless force, so fierce its whirr and pounding, "minds not the timid, minds not the weeper or prayer, the old man beseeching the young man, that does not let the child's voice be heard, nor the mother's entreaties. So loud the drums beat. Blaring are the bugles."

Then Ralph Vaughan Williams introduces the theme of Reconciliation, reminding us of how senseless war can be. Using the words of a soldier, Vaughan Williams strikes at the center of our hearts and conscience as well as at the heart of humanity's folly:

Word over all, beautiful as the sky,
beautiful, that war and all its deeds of carnage must in time be
utterly lost,
that the hands of the sisters Death and Night incessantly softly wash
again and ever again,
this soiled world;
For my enemy is dead, a man divine as myself is dead,
I look where he lies white-face and still in the coffin – I draw near,
bend down and touch lightly with my lips the white face in the
coffin.

The enemy is dead. A man divine as myself is dead!

The truth is, Christian Engledrum was someone's enemy. Christian Engledrum was in war fighting an enemy. Both were soldiers. Both were enemies. Both were divine, as each one would know themselves to be. Therein lies the tragedy of war. We have forgotten that we belong to each other. Forgotten to Whom we belong. Forgotten that we are not enemies, but brothers and sisters. That each life is divine. That we will never be able to live in peace, if we keep on killing each other's children. To recognize that each life is divine, is to recognize that there is only One, to whom, if we turn, will provide the only source of our Still, true lasting, peace.

In the chapel at the funeral home in the Bronx is a family weeping before the coffin of Christian Engeldrum. In the home of a soldier in Iraq is a family weeping over the loss of their child, husband, wife, father or mother. It is so in every war throughout history. The sad processions of grief, watched over by the immense and silent moon that shines upon those who lie in repose and upon those with broken hearts and lives in broken pieces. Each war that we have known, reminds us that our soiled earth is in need of the soft washing that true peace can provide. That soft washing comes from the heart of God's love:

God shall wipe away all tears
and there shall be no more death
no more sorrow
no more crying
neither shall there be any more pain.
Praise the Lord
Praise the Lord
Praise the Lord.

This is the promise of the One who desires that all the people of the world be held, Still, in the One peace of that promise.

Standing before Christian Engeldrum's casket looking at his white face, like Walt Whitman, *I draw near, bend down and touch lightly with my lips the white face in the coffin*, thanking Christian Engeldrum for his sacrifice. But I have seen enough. In Thomas Jefferson's words, "I have seen enough of one war never to wish to see another." And I pray that his death was not in vain. That somehow we might all come to live in and be **Still, in One Peace**.

Chapter Nineteen

Maintaining a Sense of Humor

Life is not the way its suppose to be – it's the way it is.
Virginia Satir

A merry heart doeth good like medicine.
Proverbs 17:22

I am content in my later years. I have kept my good humor and take neither myself nor the next person seriously.
A. Einstein

President Gerald R. Ford, descending the stairs after an Air Force One flight, miscalculates the steps and tumbles to the tarmac. The clumsy fall is captured by the media, broadcast around the world and has continually been replayed in the historical reflections of the Ford presidency.

President George H. W. Bush becomes ill on the dais while attending a State Dinner in Europe. The media replays the moment he becomes sick and loses his meal in front of the heads of state.

Tripping on the hem of my clerical robe during worship, I find myself flat out, face down on the stairs leading to the chancel as the tiny glass cups in the communion trays filled with sacramental wine are tossed into the air. Following a loud gasp from the congregation, I pick myself up, with the assistance of several church members, gather my composure, and continue the communion ritual, using the Chalice for intinction rather than the individual cups distributed at the communion rail.

A very obese friend of mine is standing behind a small podium (in comparison to his size) presenting an inspirational speech on dealing with adversity. His belt buckle unexpectedly breaks, sending his pants to the floor, exposing his sail-like boxers. He picks up his pants, walks out of the room. Thirty years later his recollections are still filled with embarrassment and humiliation. He can't remove the painful experience from his mind. He can't laugh it off.

I'm speaking from the pulpit delivering an inspiring Sunday Morning sermon. The church windows are open to permit the refreshing spring breezes to flow within the sanctuary. A traffic accident on the street outside the building in Washington Heights, Manhattan results in the two drivers accosting each other with the foulest language that wafts into the sanctuary, floating on those springtime breezes. I stop speaking, since the stunned congregation has diverted its attention to the vulgarities blaring through the windows. Knowing I've lost their attention, I look toward the window, then back to my audience as the four letter words continue to assault our ears and say, "that's easy for them to say!!!!" To which the congregation bursts out in laughter!

All of us have embarrassing moments!! How do we handle them?

One billion pairs of eyes stare in bewilderment and suspense as the world observes a technological glitch that prevents one of the tripod legs of the Olympic Torch caldron from rising from the floor of the center of the Vancouver 2010 Olympic Arena, as cast members stand frozen in place, wondering what to do as the failed hydraulic lift threatens to mar the highly anticipated igniting of the Olympic flame. I imagine the horror of the production staff, stage crew and set designers as the spectacular theatrical production of the opening ceremonies comes to a standstill, as the two beams of the torch rise into position while a gapping hole at center stage reveals the technological defect.

The disappointment caused by the failure was made tolerable by reflecting on the events earlier in the day, when the world watched a young athlete die on a practice run, making this catastrophic production glitch, pale in the remembrance of the Olympic athlete who lost his life preparing to compete in the Olympic Games. While the breakdown resulted in frustration, nothing could compare to the tragedy of the death of an athlete earlier that day.

The juxtaposition of tragedy and technological disappointment helped focus my thoughts on what really matters.

I once heard a comparison between a problem and an inconvenience as it related to "lumps." A lump in oatmeal, for some people, is an inconvenience, especially when the person eating Quaker Oatmeal likes a smooth, creamy consistency. But a lump, revealed in a breast following a mammogram diagnosis, is a real "problem" as that person is now confronted with a major physical condition and life-threatening crisis.

An athlete dies during practice. *That's* a major *problem*. An hydraulic lift malfunctions. That's nothing more than an *inconvenience*. How you handle the situation will determine how you approach the setback or catastrophe, in either case.

This becomes clearer when once again a billion pairs of eyes watch the parade of athletes at the closing ceremonies of the Olympic Games. All eyes are transfixed on the center of the arena. The floor opens, exposing the gaping reminder of the failed hydraulic lift just two weeks before at the opening ceremonies.

Suddenly, a figure emerges from the chasm, climbing out, in a clown's costume.

The audience, viewing the clown at close range from the giant video screens located throughout the stadium, and the worldwide audience watch in amazement, as the failure and flaw of two weeks prior is turned into a humorous moment, an opportunity, through humor and jest, not to make light of the original malfunction, but to affirm, that through humor, we can deal with our problems. We can try again. Turn our problems into opportunities and not take too seriously our defeats and failures. We can develop solution-oriented perspectives about life and its circumstances.

The clown stands at the open abyss, and in mime helps to raise the third support beam of the Olympic torch.

Virginia Satir said, "Life is not the way it's supposed to be – it's the way it is."

How we handle that life – this *"it's the way it is"* life, when life is not the way it is supposed to be, will determine how we go through life and its experiences so that we wind up in a still, place of peace, having maintained our dignity and self-control, rather than blowing our cool and surrendering to our circumstances.

Researchers Greenberg and Arakawa, conducting a corporate survey on project management asked the question, "When a problem crops up on my project, is my project manager able to help me come up with solutions?" What steps are initiated when the problems arise?" Here is what was concluded:

Managers who maintain a positive perspective don't turn setbacks into catastrophes.

They don't fly off the handle. Emotions are controlled.

They recognize what is in their sphere of influence and what is not.

The problem is discussed as an opportunity.

They provide a solution-oriented perspective.

(Dr. Maynard Bruaman, **Focus On Positive Leadership When Things Go Wrong**, Margaret Greenberg and Dana Arakawa. September 10, 2010 Accounting Web)

Gene Perret, writer for comedian Bob Hope shared an article in *Toastmaster* magazine, describing do's and don'ts of those who find themselves in difficult situations in the often glitch filled performances:

Don't blow your cool
Do maintain your dignity
Don't surrender to the situation
Do your best under any circumstances
Don't continually refer to the problem
Do keep your sense of humor.
Keep your sense of humor!

(Gene Perret, Toastmaster International Magazine, **Do's and Don'ts of When Things Go Wrong,** January 2006)

Keeping it will keep you in a Still, calm, place.

Kathryn Rose Gerty wrote an article on Laughter that reduces stress and says, "The studies prove in measurable ways that laughter does soothe the mind and restore the body. Levity boosts resilience in the face of all manner of assault. Mirth, especially when directed at ourselves, imparts a sense of control, puts distance between us and our pain, gives us perspective, relieves tension, allows us to take a break."

In the same article Kathryn Gerty says that Dr. Kuhn, author of The Fun Factor says,

a walk in the funny side shows that laughter
reduces the level of stress hormones
perks up the immune system
relaxes muscles
clears the respiratory tract
increases circulation
eases perceived pain

(Dr. Clifford Kuhn, MD, **The Fun Factor**: Unleashing the Power of Humor, Sept 1, 2003)

Gerty continues to say, "Feel-good endorphins flow, blood

pressure settles down, increased oxygen to the brain revs up creativity. Laughter stimulates and soothes. It reduces arrhythmias". When you laugh you let fresh air into your mind and sunshine into your soul.

Some experiences in life are extremely painful and cause severe wounds. They are not a laughing matter by any means. Nor can you simply laugh them off or away. But through humor, you can utilize the Physiology of Mirth, to handle the pressures, fears, glitches and real trauma of life, with a spirit that is resilient.

I am always amazed how the human spirit can go on living after life's most incredible, painful experiences. A smile of remembrance, a laughter that comes from recollecting happy times and funny moments, when a loved one has died, soothes our pain. Amid the pain, trauma, and chaos you can laugh at life, simply because you realize that "life is not the way it is suppose to be – it's simply the way it is."

Don't ever lose your sense of humor. Let mirth heal and hold you. Don't lose your cool. Maintain your dignity. Don't surrender to chaos. Don't continually refer to the problem. Keep your sense of humor. Remember the clown that appeared on the center of the arena during the closing ceremonies of the Olympic Games. He is a reminder that the production team of the ceremonies did not succumb to devastating circumstances. But through levity, humor, mirth, a solution-oriented perspective, turned a setback into a new opportunity. It was not only symbolic of athletic prowess to try, try again after each failure. It was a symbol of the prowess of levity and the human spirit to rise above the glitches that come our way.

Humor, will keep you *Still, in One Peace*. Laugh a little at yourself. Learn the difference between a lump in your oatmeal and a lump in the breast. Don't take yourself too seriously, but be serious about allowing humor to bring you to the place where you can be *Still, in One Peace*.

Resource: Kathryn Gerty, Article on Laughter

Chapter Twenty

Grace – I Hope He Stays a While – Shirley Valentine

Joe, would you like to join me for a drink?...
Shirley Valentine, The Movie

Yes, I've fallen in love – fallen in love with the idea of living...
Shirley Valentine, The Movie

It takes a lot of courage to release the familiar and seemingly secure to embrace the new. But there is no real security in what is no longer meaningful. There is more security in the adventurous and exciting, for in movement there is life – and with change there is power.
Alan Cohen

For the past twenty-eight years I have vacationed each summer in Mykonos, Greece. My hotel is located a few miles outside the "Chora," city of Mykonos, in a small hamlet called Ornos Beach, located within walking distance from Agios Ionis, a quaint, quiet village where the movie Shirley Valentine was filmed in 1989.

In 2008 ten members of my family traveled together celebrating the occasion of my parents' 65th Anniversary. We spent two weeks on the Aegean Islands and visiting Mom's family in Athens and our family homestead in Nemouta, my grandfather's birthplace near the Peloponnesian town of Olympia, the site of the original Hellenistic games.

My cousin Valerie insisted on visiting the beach hotel where Shirley Valentine was filmed to reenact the scene from the movie where Shirley Valentine enjoys a glass of wine at a small bistro table on the sand at the edge of the Aegean water, as she watched the sunset.

From the moment I first visited Mykonos, I fell in love with Greek island life. I fully understood the emotional dynamics that the character, Shirley Valentine, played by Pauline Collins, was experiencing. The film was released in 1989, five years after I began my own love affair with the Aegean gem, the diamond among the Cyclades Islands. By the time the movie was released, I had become acquainted with the life-changing experience that one can find in Mykonos.

The plot of the movie, however, was not only about having a "love affair with living." It would also be a poignant expression of grace and forgiveness that brings one's heart to a moment of self-discovery, to the still, peaceful place within the heart that is filled with grace. This is not just a heartwarming movie. It is a heart-changing moment in the lives of anyone seeking to find peace and contentment within themselves.

Shirley Valentine Bradshaw touches the deep places of the human heart. She is a bored housewife in England who suffers the insensitive abuses of her domineering, demanding husband Joe, and a family who pays her little attention to the point that she talks to the "wall" in her kitchen in order to have someone, even if it be a blank, unresponsive "wall" to talk to.

When her friend Jane wins a trip for two to Mykonos, Shirley accepts Jane's invitation to join her, only after the continued abuse of her husband, who in one scene throws a plate of chips and eggs into her lap at the kitchen table because Shirley did not prepare the normal "steak" dinner on a Thursday night. Her husband says, "We have eggs and chips on Tuesday. We have steak on THURSDAY!!!!." Shirley aches for the "girl who used to be me." She's now a 42-year-old housewife with two grown children and a husband she feels has fallen out of love with her. She has had enough, and seeks the adventure of finding her life.

In her conversations with the "wall" she wonders if she has made the right choices in life. Pauline Collins, who plays Shirley, represents all of us who question our own lives, in this heartwarming, sentimental story. Throwing the plate of food into her lap is the last straw and Shirley leaves a note on the pantry door for Joe, announcing that she has gone and left him for a two-week holiday in Greece.

Shirley's friend Jane begins a romantic liaison with a man she meets on the flight to Greece. Upon her arrival in Mykonos, Jane leaves Shirley stranded to fend for herself for a few days. Only Shirley begins exploring the island and discovers the small hotel on the beach, where I have had dinner many times during my Mykonos vacations.

She asks Costas, the owner of the hotel, to help fulfill the dream she has – a dream to drink wine by the sea. He moves a small table and chair by the sea. Where she sits and reflects about her life. About being alone. About her future. He invites her to join him the next day on his boat, but she shyly reneges on the invitation, somewhat aware of the reputation of "Greek men," though he feeds her a line that he will not take advantage of her. She agrees.

The morning of their outing on the boat, Jane returns but Shirley leaves her stranded with the other tourists and goes out on the boat with Costas to a remote coastline cove where they skinny dip in the turquoise water, and where she eventually gives in to her impulses, making love with Costas on the rocking boat, as the tiny waves, swirl with orgasmic flow.

When Jane hears the story, she accuses Shirley of falling in love, of having a fling on her Grecian holiday. Shirley confronts her and says, "Yes, I've fallen in love – I've fallen in love with the idea of living."

"Yes," everyone falls in love on their holiday. But we've all got to go home!" Jane says.

When it comes time to return to England the two women arrive at the airport in Mykonos, but Shirley quickly decides to stay, leaving Jane to take the flight alone. Shirley returns to her hotel to stay. Arriving at the taverna, she finds Costas feeding the same line, word for word, to another woman, the same line she was fed from him when she arrived at the restaurant. Costas, embarrassed by the encounter that has revealed his womanizing, does not suffer the rage or rebuke of Shirley Valentine. Instead she gracefully says, "Costas, it's alright. I understand. I'm only back here to have a job while I stay longer in Greece."

Throughout the film there is a visual transformation of the physical appearance of Shirley Valentine as having a love affair with life, she regains a love and respect of herself, a respect that transforms her essence and spirit.

Joe is at the airport in England with flowers to give his wife, but he is greeted by Jane who breaks the news to him that she has gone crazy, and has fallen in love. Joe calls the island incessantly and becomes increasingly desperate for her as he realizes that she has become more content with her new life.

In a conversation with his son, the son tells his father that he is so disappointed in his father's inability to "go after his wife." to fight for her. To win her back. The son's words compel Joe to go to Greece. Shirley receives a telegram that he is to arrive on the island. Afraid of the encounter, Costas makes an excuse to be away from the hotel.

It is the closing scene of the move that is filled with all the aspects of grace, understanding and affection. It is a moment of peace and love, symbolic of forgiveness and acceptance.

Up until this point Shirley on her path of self-discovery, makes anyone identifying with her, realize that "it takes a lot of courage to release the familiar and seemingly secure to embrace the new. But there is no real security in what is no longer meaningful. There is more security in the adventurous and exciting, for in movement there is life – and with change there is power." Shirley Valentine had the courage to release the familiar and seemingly secure to embrace the new. To embrace the new life she was finding within herself. To embrace the idea that she had lost who she once was and perhaps to understand that even her husband had lost the same love and passion of life that he once had.

We watch Joe walking down the narrow roadway, with suitcase in hand, toward the waterfront hotel. He looks lost, alone, nervous, a man in search as well, for something, someone, he realized he had lost. I've walked this same road many times in my visits to Mykonos. And to my journey within.

Shirley is seated at her bistro table on the sand, looking radiant and stylish. Remember, she had asked Costas to set the table at this place at the beginning of the movie because she wanted to drink wine on a table by the sea, as she began her "falling in love with living" excursion. And now the table is set again, for this sacramental moment.

The bistro table becomes symbolic of wine by the water, by the sunset and the warmth of the end of the day when all of our life comes to be still in the remains of the peaceful day.

Joe walks by, not recognizing his wife behind the sunglasses, as she sits there in radiant loveliness.

Shirley turns to him and calls "Joe!"

He stops, Turns. Their eyes connect and she removes her glasses.

"I didn't recognize you," he says.

"I know," she responds.

"I use to be the wife! The mother. But now I'm Shirley Valentine again!"

Then she says to Joe, "Joe, would you like to join me for a drink?"

He sits down at the bistro table, with the wine glasses by the sea and the movie ends with the romantic musical theme of contentment and peace that underscores the life that Shirley has found and the grace that she offers to her husband. It is as if they meet for the first time. It is a moment of recognition of love that they have shared through the years. It is a recognition of the chance to still find something new of passion, a life, of love. Of perhaps, finding each other once again. It is a quiet, intimate recognition of tender forgiveness.

As I watch this closing scene, I recall the words that Shirley says as she watches his approach down the narrow road to the hotel:

"Here he comes. I hope he stays a while. He needs a holiday. He needs to have the sun wash over his skin and to swim in water as deep as forever."

It is such a loving statement of grace, compassion, forgiveness and hope. It can only come from a heart that does not reside in resentments and accusations. A heart that is non-judgmental and critical.

The invitation to join her for a drink of wine is a sacramental invitation. A sacred moment by the Aegean Sea. It is an invitation of reconciliation. An invitation of acceptance and caring. Of compassion and forgiveness. It is an invitation to share in a new sense of joy. To share a love newly discovered. To rekindle the passions that were lost. To dream of a new life. An invitation to let grace touch the heart. An invitation that accepts our own imperfection and is tolerant of another's. They share new words, see new beginnings. Words of acceptance. Where regrets are released. Where no insults are hurled. The table on the beach is such a contrast from the table in their home in England where chips and eggs were tossed and harsh words cruelly and insensitively expressed. Here, at this table, they both hold love. They bring their lives to a place of peace.

Shirley had fallen in love with living. It was here that Joe was about to begin that same love affair with living.

We see them sitting together, *Still, in One Peace*, as the credits of the movie are displayed on the screen. It is true! It takes a lot of courage to release the familiar and seemingly secure, to embrace the new. To embrace the security of being Still, in the one love and peacefulness of the life God gives us to enjoy. We find life in Him when we find ourselves Still, in the One peace of life – in falling in love with living. By loving one another.

They were both attempting to find new meaning in life. To be their true selves once again. To be Shirley Valentine. To be Joe Bradshaw At this table they found more security in the adventurous excitement of the fullness of living. For in moving to this place where life is found in the stillness and peacefulness of all its gifts, they found the power to change. Being still, in that peace, allows us to find those moments that allow us to fall in love with living. Be still, in that peace. And live! And love!

Resource: MoviePhonePlots/Internet/Shirley Valentine

Chapter Twenty-One

The Sabbath of the Deeper Sea

When winds are raging o'er the upper ocean, and waves are tossed
wild with an angry roar,
It's said, far down beneath the wild commotion
That peaceful stillness reigns forevermore.
Harriet Beecher Stowe

Currently in film production is a new movie about HMS Titanic. Produced in England, the story documents the real life characters aboard the ill-fated trip, 1500 of whom lost their lives after the ocean liner, on its maiden voyage from England to New York City, struck an iceberg, sinking off the coast of Newfoundland on April 15, 1912. The story has fascinated us for 101 years.

James Cameron, producer of the Academy Award winning movie Titanic, captures the images of the ship residing in its ocean grave two and a half miles beneath the surface of the Atlantic Ocean. No matter how often we view the bow of Titanic, its eerie stillness conveys a peaceful solitude as the ship rests on the ocean floor. We cannot grasp the shocking, terrifying trauma that occurred on the surface that clear, cold, star-studded night, as pandemonium filled the desperate men, women and children trying to save their lives, as the vessel slipped beneath the surface of the mirror-like sea reflecting the celestial brightness of that quiet darkness, during one of Maritime's greatest catastrophes.

The Titanic in its ocean grave compels me to ponder its now still, repose of peace. Still, in one peace, far beneath the tumult of the horror on that night in 1912, when it plunged, in pieces, to its final resting place, in the still silence of the ominous ocean. The remembrance of this disaster creates a contrast and conflict in the mind that relives its horror. The scene is a contrast of panic, fear and death on the surface of the sea and the muted stillness and tranquility of the ocean's embrace, as if the ocean holds and protects the ship in its tumult-free waters two and a half miles below the surface, where only temperate currents ebb and flow.

I love the personalities of the waves when swimming in the ocean, jumping over expanding crests, or diving under surging breakers. I experience the temperament of the sea, from serene, moderate waves, or lake-like tranquility when calm breezes traverse the surface of the water. Or those aggressive foam-frothing waves kicked up by 10- to 12-foot rollers that create Jacuzzi, whirlpools that invigorate and stimulate the body.

There is an art to navigating waves. You cannot merely stand up, confront or bully the breakers head on. They will send you tumbling, in the agitating, churning surf unable to gain a sense of direction, of which way is up or down, as you are caught within their ferocious strength. As the waves consecutively roll in, you cannot simply bend lower, thinking the surf will wash over you, leaving you standing there stimulated and massaged by the swirling water. You just get walloped in the face, gasping for air, battered and beaten, struggling to find a place to come up landing on two feet, only to find yourself physically fatigued.

There is a way to handle the forcible waves when besieged by their unrelenting swells. You dive under them. And you dive as deep as you can. In fact, I dive under them and lay on the bottom, flat on the sandy floor of the surf. I open my eyes and watch the waves roll over head, with the foam and bubbles creating patterns and swirls above, while I lie securely on the bottom till the wave passes and I can come up for air, ready to catch the next wave.

This is an interesting image. Lying prostrate on the sandy bottom while the torrents and currents roll over head. It is a reminder of what we need to do when life comes surging over us. To lay low, taking a position as far down below the surface you can go. To be still, deep down, low, still, where there is peace below the torrents that could otherwise cause us to be broken in pieces.

When winds are raging o'er the upper ocean,
and waves are tossed wild with an angry roar,
It's said, far down beneath the wild commotion,
that peaceful stillness reigns forevermore.

Far, far beneath, noise of tempests falls silent,
and silver waves lie ever peacefully,
and no storm, however fierce or violent,
disturbs the Sabbath of that deeper sea.

So to the heart that knows Your love, O Father,
There is a temple sacred evermore,
and all life's angry voices causing bother
die in hushed silence at its peaceful door.

Far, far away, the roars of strife fall silent,
and loving thoughts rise ever peacefully,
and no storm, however fierce or violent,
disturbs the soul that dwells, O Lord in Thee.

(Harriet Beecher Stowe)

The Sabbath of that deeper sea!! This is a kind way of remembering the horror of that April night in 1912, as we observe the Titanic at the ocean floor held in the "Sabbath of that deeper sea." There is a temple sacred evermore, at the Sabbath of that deeper sea, a hushed silence of peace at its peaceful door. No storm, however fierce or violent can disturb the soul that rests in that Sabbath place of peace. It is in that place that we find ourselves, *Still, in One Peace.*

That peaceful door, to that Sabbath rest, need not be a church, a temple or mosque. It might be a place where we step into a cathedral forest, or stand at the rim of a grand canyon. It might be the place where we lay low, beneath the waves and torrents of life, in a meadow field, or mountain range. Or lying on the grass in our own backyard, watching the clouds drift overhead. It might be the solitude of an armchair in our living room after a hectic day, in contemplative thought or quiet nap. It might be sitting on a park bench or swinging on a swing. It might be in the holding of someone's hand who offers safe harbor while the tempest waves of life swirl around us. It might be in listening to inspiring music, or engaged in a devotional, inspirational book, touched by a meaningful scene in a movie, or hearing a reassuring word from a friend, or hearing your name spoken as you are welcomed at an AA meeting. It might be during a morning sunrise or evening sunset, or watching the full rising moon changing from orange to bright white as it ascends into the sky. It might be in the arms of a friend, spouse or loved one who holds you within their encouraging love and forgiveness.

Nothing can disturb the sacred Sabbath of a heart that finds itself resting at the door that leads to being *Still, in One Peace.* Find it deep, below the wild commotion. Where the angry voices of life are lost in hushed silence. It is the place where loving thoughts rise ever peacefully.

Chapter Twenty-Two

Simplify, Simplify, Alone in a Little Cell

Ah to be alone in a little cell with nobody near me, beloved that pilgrimage before the last pilgrimage to death...
Anonymous Poems by Irish Monks of the 8th-15th Centuries.

As you simplify your life, the laws of the universe will be simpler; solitude will not be solitude, poverty will not be poverty, nor weakness weakness.
Henry David Thoreau

I would rather sit on a pumpkin and have it all to myself, than be crowded on a velvet cushion.
Henry David Thoreau

Simplify, simplify.
Henry David Thoreau

Sometimes, in a summer morning, having taken my accustomed bath, I sat in my sunny doorway from sunrise till noon, rapt in a reverie, amidst the pines and hickories and sumacs, in undisturbed solitude and stillness, while the birds sang around or flitted noiseless through the house, until by the sun falling in at my west window, or the noise of some traveler's wagon on the distant highway, I was reminded of the lapse of time.
Henry David Thoreau

Ah, to be content in a little cell with nobody near me! To be happy and gratified in all things! To be undisturbed in solitude and stillness with a strong sense of deep, inner peace. To be *Still, in One Peace.*

This is where I find my life right now. Like Thoreau, on a summer morning, sitting in a sunny doorway from sunrise till noon, rapt in all the shades of life. Surrounded by pines and hickories, in undisturbed solitude and stillness, while a bird sings, filling my life with music and hope.

Time goes by. I am content. Content in all things. Content with "nobody near me" does not mean I find true happiness when secluded from others. Or estranged from the busy, chaotic mundane routine of living. It means I am content with who I am, not needing something external from my soul, or someone near to me, to determine my optimism or fashion my world.

My pilgrimage in life has led to the place where sun falling in at the west window of my heart reminds me that I am gifted with the designs, textures, colors and lights and promises of all that surrounds me – that brings harmony, peace, contentment and purpose – without the infusion of things or intrusion of others to determine who I am.

It is that Still, One peace that gives me my self-worth. That slows my search for something else to fulfill me on this pilgrimage before that last pilgrimage of my life. Moving nearer to that still, One place of peace, the pilgrimage reminds me to simplify my life – to simplify it with stillness and peace. To lean my life, position my life, in that One peace.

My life and world looks so different when viewed from this "sunny doorway" of my spirit and soul. I would rather sit on this porch of my soul, or on a "pumpkin and have it all to myself, than be crowded on a velvet cushion." My perspective of life is fundamentally clarified by reclining in this doorway, this threshold from which I perceive life and myself more simply. More simply content. More still, in peace. The view of "pines and hickories and sumacs, of streams and clouds and moon glow, reminds me to "simplify, simplify," so that the view from the doorway of my soul is that of solitude and stillness, for which I have been searching above all things.

The more I realize that I find my solitude, stillness and contentment with having less, the more I discover that I am rapt with everything that provides me with more – more of life, more of wholeness, more of healing, more of imagination, more of contemplation, more of stillness, more of peace. More of others.

The view from my summer morning porch, or my winter season seclusions, or springtime wanderings, or fall time reflections, reveal a pathway that leads to an invitation to discover the solitude and stillness through my soul-ful wonderings among the pines and hickories, in the meadows of my solitude and stillness. Here I find the breathtaking views of love and life, as my life resides **Still, in One Peace**. Becoming more content with less, the more simplified I make my life, the more I am able to open my life, my spirit, to issues, concerns and needs that exist beyond selfish concerns. The world, others, become important.

The view has changed from the sunlit porch of my imagination, as seen through those spiritual eyes as the physical eyes have grown dim. Views that have changed my perspective on living, and sharpened my awareness of other things that matter beyond the "velvet cushions" of my life.

There are so many views we can hold of life. I like the view from the soul's porch the best. But there are other kinds of views:

Penthouse views overlooking Central Park. Views from porches of homes overlooking golf courses. Aspen, Colorado Cabin Houses facing majestic snow-capped mountains and ski lodges. High-rise apartments with a view over the New York City Skyline. Beachfront mansions that have a panorama of the Pacific Ocean or Shore homes that scan the Atlantic. The Hampton getaways on Long Island, or the country estates and horse farms in Bedminster, New Jersey. These are all images that entice us in Architectural Digest magazines. I dream of residing in one of those someday. I used to say, "I'll get my boat, seashore home or country estate, when my "book comes in!"' But the starving artists syndrome holds true for literary writers as well as actors and painters. I still don't have that home. But my life is content.

Is the real art of living found in the art of living as featured in Architectural Digest, where "we can visit the home of the stars, see the estates for sale, discover exotic properties on the French Riviera, the Aegean Islands, St. Tropez and Capri?" All the ads say, "We can peek into the homes of the stylish and famous, discover their private retreats, find those sophisticated spaces and serene oases. Vacation homes with remarkable views of Santorini cliffs in Greece. Homes for the affluent and style conscious." We can view properties around the world represented by Sothebys or be awestruck by the finest of interior design, trends and fashions. We equate wealth with space! Interior space! Landscapes and acres of property. Big kitchens, spacious master bedrooms, three-car garages and tennis courts. And Olympic-size swimming pools.

But what about our inner space? The inner design of that space once we step over the threshold of our souls. What resides there? Is it stillness and solitude? Peace? Ah, how the awareness of these palatial views change when I'm on the subway, commuting on the elevated tracks that run through the apartment dwellings on city streets, rumbling, roaring through their corridors so close to the tenement buildings, that you can reach out the windows of the subway car and grab the curtains from flats on hot summer days as the train squeals past the city dwellers' bedroom windows on torrid days. What a view some people have – of life. Of themselves. It is not always one of majestic landscapes featured in magazines. Yet, these are the city dwellers to whom I minister providing hope for their souls and peace for their hearts. Whether in our stately homes or low-income housing, the hearts that live there long for something to sustain them with hope and peace.

I listen to conversations of older people as they anticipate making life comfortable in their remaining years. I hear what some might call an eccentric concept about "scaling down." "We don't need all these rooms anymore!" So we do what Henry David Thoreau suggests: Simplify! Simplify!

We need not wait till our senior years to realize we need to scale down. When I was younger, I use to go to boat shows at the Javits Center in New York where sales people approached me with the question, "Do you want to upgrade?" Bigger boats!!

Now, I'm thinking about "scaling down!" Simplify! Simplify! In a sense I am not talking about scaling back, scaling down. But upgrading to a level of "simplify." Simplify. Of moving to a deeper level of inner peace and solitude. Upgrading my life to a deeper place and purpose. A truer purpose. Ah, to be alone in a little cell, upgrading to simplifying my living space within the interior of my spirit and soul. I'll be moving on up, like the television theme song of the comedy The Jeffersons, but not to some apartment on Park Avenue in the sky.

There is nothing wrong with having the type of lifestyles mentioned above. There is something wrong, missing in life, when we cannot find the inner peace within the interior design of our souls. When we have attained much, and have sacrificed solace, solitude and contentment within our hearts to attain it all. I heard a woman seriously encourage her daughter that when she marries, she should snag a "rich guy!" "Why so?" I asked, as we ate at a picnic table in her backyard. She said, "Because when you divorce you get half of everything!"

Warren Buffet, one of the world's richest men, has kept it modest with his house. He still resides in the gray stucco home he bought in 1958 for $31,500. This has something to say about being content in your interior space. This says something about the view he has from the porch of his soul, where in his privileged, yet simplified living he has allowed himself to be philanthropic with the needs he sees beyond the front porch of his home and soul.

I admit, I wish I had assets that would permit me to live more comfortably without worrying about bills, debts or unforeseen expenses of those rainy day moments. Yet, as I look at my life, my parents and my grandparents' lives when they were living, we never had much in the form of salaries, savings or stocks. But we worked hard. We enjoy life. Love fills our home. There was always a good meal on the table. Our home was and is filled with family and company, with happy memories, joyous holidays, special occasions. We were raised in homes that found deep joy in faith and worship through the life of our church. Within our interior space, was the One who gave us a deeper sense of peace. We have no regrets that occupy space in our family scrapbooks, no anger residing in dark closets. We've been blessed with much.

Ah, to be alone in a little cell. This thought comes from the Hermit Songs, a cycle of songs for voice and piano written by Samuel Barber in 1953. The songs take as their basis a collection of anonymous poems written by Irish Monks and scholars of the 8th to 15th centuries. My favorite song is "The Desire of Hermitage." The desire for a simple life, close to nature, animals and God. Robin Flour said, "It was not only that these scribes lived by the destiny of their dedication to an environment of wood and sea; it was because they brought with that environment an eye washed miraculously clear by a continual spiritual exercise that they had that strange vision of natural things in an almost unnatural purity." Thus they were able to write:

Ah! To be alone in a little cell with nobody near me,
beloved that pilgrimage before the last pilgrimage to death,
singing the passing hours to cloudy heavens;
feeding upon dry bread and water from the cold spring.
That will be an end to evil when I am alone in a lovely
little corner among tombs.
Far from the houses of the great.
Ah. To be all alone in a little cell,

To be alone, all alone
Alone I came into the world
Alone I shall go from it.

This is a wonderful poem about finding stillness, in One peace. The simplicity of living with bread and water from the cold spring. Content with simple things. However, there appears within the text a strange, awkward line:

"That will be an end to evil when I am alone in a lovely little corner among tombs."

Among tombs! How puzzling the thought. Among tombs. What a view of living in the tiny little cell. Everyone wants a room with a view! But a room with a view that looks at tombs?

It made me think of a view from the windows of a friend's home. A stark contrast of the views mentioned in those Architectural Digest estates and villas overlooking beautiful landscapes.

My friend's home has a small backyard. On the other side of the wall behind their home, is a large cemetery with endless rows of tombstones. Not particularly an inspiring or stunning view to have from your front window or while you're eating at the dining room table.

But the view inspires me, in a profound way, when I look at it philosophically. Spiritually.

A view of tombs.

I stand at that window thinking: We come into the world with nothing. We go out with nothing. I suddenly find myself looking at tombs from my simple cell, the simple cell of my body. My life. I become acquainted with my mortality. I realize life has a time span, a parenthesis around it in the course of time. I too, live among the tombs. In my little cell. I have a beginning. An end. I am content to be far away from the houses of the great. Content with simplifying my life. Simplify. Simplify. Scaling down in order that I might upgrade my awareness to be content with simplicity. "'Tis the gift to be simple, the gift to be free, tis the gift to turn around where you ought to be." I look at my life as I peer at the tombstones and am reminded that to live life fully is to live life simply. I am happy to be alive. With my little space here on earth. My little cell.

There is a story written by Allan Seager in 1934 that tells of the view that we have through the windows of life, as we view life through the window of our souls.

Two elderly bed-ridden men shared a room in a hospice. One of them had a bed next to a window, and would sit and describe in loving detail to his friend the children playing in the sunshine, the dogs loping in the park and all the things of the joys of life that appeared out his window. Though he loved the descriptions, the other man soon became sick with jealousy. This went on for months, until one night the man by the window suddenly groaned and called to his pal, "Ooh, you've got to ring for help, I don't think I'll last the night." The other fellow reached for the alarm, but then thought, "If he goes, I'll get the bed by the window." So he lay back and ignored the moaning.

Sadly, in the morning, the staff found the poor old man had died, but they reassured his pal that they'd soon have some more company for him. "I must have the bed next to the window!" he said. The nurses explained it would be easier if he stayed put, but he angrily insisted. So they lifted him to the other bed. Expectantly, he levered himself up and peered through the window – to see a solid brick wall of the building outside the window.

We realize in this story that what the deceased man saw out the window were visions of life he had imagined through the contentment that he found in his spirit and soul. In the cell of his own room, in the attitudes of his mind and spirit, he saw a beautiful world all around him.

Henry David Thoreau was right:

"As you simplify your life, the laws of the universe will be simpler; solitude will not be solitude, poverty will not be poverty, nor weakness, weakness."

You will simply be content. At peace. *Still, in One Peace.* Regardless of your status or state, your mansion or your cabin porch, or even from your nursing home bed, you will be richly blessed, as you view life through the windows of your soul.

There will always be a tension in our lives between the desires of the heart – the desire for those upgraded needs that drive us, compel us or tempt us and the desire, the deep inner longing for simplified places that provide true solitude and peace. We are reminded of that tension through another Monk, Cuthbert of Lindisfarne (d687) Monk in Scotland:

"If I could live in a tiny dwelling on a rock in the ocean, surrounded by the waves of the sea and cut off from the sight and sound of everything else, I would still not be free of the cares of this passing world, or from the fear that somehow the love of money might still come and snatch me away."

I think this is an ongoing conflict for all of us.

When you take your "accustomed bath" in the morning and sit at the sunny doorway or window at the kitchen table having your morning coffee, make yourself aware, from sunrise till noon, that you are rapt in a reverie, in undisturbed solitude and stillness. Hear a bird sing around you or let it flit noiseless through the house of your soul and let the sun come falling in at the west window of your heart. Simplify. Simplify. Ah, be thankful to be alone in a little cell, your personal space, where you live and know that you are **Still, *in One Peace.*** It might not be an Architectural Digest moment. But it will be a moment filled with many blessings. Know that you are truly rich! That your life and world is truly beautiful.

Chapter Twenty-Three

Prayer

Oh, in the time of silence when man remains alone, abandoned when he does not hear Thy voice, it seems to him doubtless that the separation must last forever. Oh, in the time of silence when man consumes himself in the desert in which he does not hear Thy voice, it seems to him doubtless that it is completely extinguished. It is merely a moment of silence in an intimacy of conversation. Bless then this silence as Thy word to man; grant that he never forgets that Thou speakest also when Thou art silent... that Thou guidest by Thy voice and that Thou dost instruct by Thy silence.
Soren Kierkegaard

Be soft in your practice. Think of the method as a fine silvery stream, not a raging waterfall. Follow the stream, have faith in its course. It will go its own way, meandering here, trickling there. It will find the grooves, the cracks, the crevices. Just follow it. Never let it out of your sight. It will take you...
Sheng-yen

Blessed are the single-hearted, for they shall enjoy much peace. If you refuse to be hurried and pressed, if you stay your soul on God, nothing can keep you from that clearness of spirit which is life and peace. In that stillness you will know what His will is.
Amy Carmichael

Bring yourself back to the point quite gently. And even if you do nothing during the whole of your hour but bring your heart back a thousand times, though it went away every time you brought it back, your hour would be very well employed.
St. Francis De Sales, on Meditation

When life becomes more than you can stand, kneel.

Anonymous

That prayer has great power which a person makes with all his might. It makes a sour heart sweet, a sad heart merry, a poor heart rich, a foolish heart wise, a timid heart brave, a sick heart well, a blind heart full of sight, a cold heart ardent. It draws down the great God into the little heart; it drives the hungry soul up into the fullness of God; it brings together two lovers, God and the soul, in a wondrous place where they speak much of love.

Mechthild of Magdeburg

There is truth in the saying, "**Seven days** without prayer makes one WEAK. In order for us to find that still place of lasting peace, we must pray. Yet this discipline is one of the weakest, derelict places of our spiritual journey. Imagine a month, a season, and a year without prayer. If we all have a soul, what if we leave it unattended? What happens when there is nothing of love spoken there? Do we leave God always standing alone, up against the wall of our soul, yearning for our approach with prayerful hands to dance? Or does the deficiency of prayer in our life make God the jilted lover?

Thus we turn now to prayer. To the discipline that brings together two lovers – God and the soul. Prayer connects them as one. Attaches our hearts together. In a wondrous place where they speak much of love. Where miracles happen. Where peace abides. Where faith is lived. Where hope encourages. Where life is changed. It is the place of deep, still, lasting peace. We find a moment of silence in an intimacy of conversation. God speaks when God is silent. God listens when we wander from that intimate place of wondrous love, time and again. A thousand times returning. We bring our hearts back, in prayer, to contemplation, inquisitiveness and attentiveness.

When we realize life is too much for us to stand, kneel we

must. Without kneeling in that intimate, wondrous place in prayer that brings together two lovers, God and the soul, our spirits remain weak and God's efforts powerless. In that time of silence, in that place of prayer, we remain alone – ah, to be alone in a little cell, with no one near me, except God! In prayer, we find ourselves, alone, with God. Without prayer, we find ourselves alone! Consumed by the desert heats of our making, concerns like worry, fear, anxiety, stress, pain, suffering, care.

If God seems sometimes nowhere to be found, silent, distant, uncaring, "pray earnestly the more." Through prayer we drive our hungry soul up to God, even if we feel God is unconcerned about our needs, or silent to our meditation. Stay your soul on God. God speaks, guides and instructs when God is silent. God's voice in not "completely extinguished."

God's voice is not always heard like a raging waterfall, flowing powerfully, thunderously speaking to us on waves of cascading assurances over the rocky, precarious cliffs of our lives. We feel the separation, the silence. We doubt God's sincerity. God's presence. We fall away. Turn away. Run away. Doubt. Mistrust. Become resistant. Hardened. Separated.

But we must remain soft. Returning to the place of prayer quite gently. Expecting. Longing. Pleading. Returning time and time again, a thousand times, after having wondered away a thousand times, discovering in that prayerful return that our prayers bring God down into the little heart, and drives our hungry soul up in to the fullness of God. It brings two lovers together, God and the soul, where they pray and speak much of love.

His voice comes not as a raging waterfall. Sometimes it comes as a silvery stream. Or a vast silence, a silence, like the density of space we feel standing on a mountain ridge at night, knowing the vast space of the gorge or valley holds all the silence in the valley like a well of solitude. The distance creates the density of silence. A silence, as they say, you can cut with a knife. The foreboding influence of silence. You can hear the stillness. Touch the silence. Hear the wind whisper through the trees.

Listen to the silence. The silvery stream. The gentle flow. The quiet water. Like a leaf, a prayer, carried on the water. Follow the stream, have faith in its course. It will go its own way, meandering here, trickling there. It will find the grooves, the cracks, the crevices. "Just follow it. Never let it out of your sight. It will take you..." Just let the silence carry you. Never let prayer out of your mind. Always utter prayers from your lips. Speak them in the silence of your soul.

Pray consistently. Earnestly. Ardently. Mightily. Such prayer has great power. Without it, Mechthild of Magdeburg says we remain sour, sad, poor, foolish, timid, sick, blind, cold. When we pray with might we make a sour heart sweet, a sad heart merry, a poor heart rich, a foolish heart wise, a timid heart brave, a sick heart well, a blind heart full of sight, a cold heart ardent.

When we don't pray we allow ourselves to be consumed in the deserts of our lives, those wilderness places, where temptations assault us and other voices claim us. God speaks, guides and instructs in the silence.

In public speaking I have learned the skill in delivery, when telling a powerful story, hopefully with life-changing possibilities, to "suspend the thought." Express it. Hold it out there. Before the mind of the listener. Give it time, through a brief moment of silence, to allow it to assimilate into the listener's mind and heart. This is called "timing." The speaker is not merely rapidly firing information or words that the hearer cannot process, like those television commercials that have those rapid fire advertisements by speakers spouting off a barrage of words within a short span of time. Those Crazy Eddie, tirade voices. All that does is drive you insane.

I'm wondering if the silence we attribute to God is indeed the "timing" the suspended thought of our Creator, who, in that wondrous place where God meets soul, allows His truth and love to flow through our minds in contemplation as we are attentive to God's word. He speaks, instructs, guides, in a moment of silence. The silence of His perfect timing. If you stay your soul on God, nothing can keep you from that clearness of spirit which is life and peace. In that stillness you will know what His will is.

The French writer Jean Paul Sartre said, not having a belief in God, postulates what it is like living without God:

"God does not see me, God does not hear me. God does not know me. You see this gap in the door? It is God. You see that hole in the ground? It is God again. Silence is God. Absence is God. God is the loneliness of man."

I do feel that if we neglect prayer in our life or abstain from it, we run the risk of adapting our lives to such a philosophy as Sartre.

I watch families pray before their meals in a restaurant. I know there is a wondrous place in their hearts and home where they speak with God, where they speak much of love.

I observe someone on the bus or train reading their Bible, prayer book, or mediations and I know there is a wondrous place in their hearts and home where they speak with God, where they speak much of love.

In hospitals, funeral homes, offices, meeting places, I see two people holding hands in prayer and I know there is a wondrous place in their hearts, in the work place, in the wellness centers where they speak with God, where they speak much of love.

I listen to the prayer of a husband for his wife and children, or a mother for the care and well-being of her home and family, and I know there is a wondrous place in their hearts and home where they speak with God, where they speak much of love.

A Chaplain in a prison cell, holds the Bible, sharing God's grace with inmates and see Chaplain and inmate, their heads bowed in prayer and I know there is a wondrous place in their hearts and in that cell where they speak with God, where they speak much of love.

Blessed are the single-hearted, the ones who find themselves in the wondrous place, where God and soul come together as lovers. "It draws down the great God into the little heart; it drives the hungry soul up into the fullness of God; it brings together two lovers, God and the soul, in a wondrous place where they speak much of love." It is the place, where our soul finds itself *Still, in God's peace.*

Keep returning there. A thousand times more. Bring your heart back a thousand times, though it went away every time you brought it back. Your hour would be very well employed. You will find yourself, *Still, in One Peace.*

Chapter Twenty-Four

How Can I Keep from Singing – God has No Religion

When the mind begins to become still, we then begin to truly see it. When you first try to stabilize and pacify the mind, initially it will become very busy because it's not accustomed to being still. In fact, it doesn't even necessarily want to become still, but it is essential to get a hold of the mind to recognize its nature. This practice is extremely important. ... Eventually you will find yourself in a state where your mind is clear and open all the time. It is just like when the clouds are removed from the sky and the sun can clearly be seen, shining all the time. This is coming close to the state of liberation, liberation from all traces of suffering. ... The truth of this practice is universal. It isn't necessary to call it a religion to practice it. Whether one is a Hindu or a Muslim or a Christian or a Buddhist simply doesn't matter. Anyone can practice this because this is the nature of the mind, the nature of everyone's mind. If you can get a handle on your mind, and pacify it in this way, you will definitely experience these results, and you will see them in your daily life situation. There is no need to put this into any kind of category, any kind of 'ism.'
Venerable Gyatrul Rinpoche. "Introduction to Buddhism"

O Krishna, the stillness of divine union which you describe is beyond my comprehension. How can the mind, which is so restless, attain lasting peace? Krishna, the mind is restless, turbulent, powerful, violent; trying to control it is like trying to tame the wind.
Bhagavad Gita

My peace I give to you, but not as the world gives, do I give it to you.
Jesus Christ

In this book I attempted to bring our mind, body and soul to a position of stillness. Still(ness), in One peace. Still, until we could see the mind. Still, until we could feel the soul. To provide encouragement to "begin to still the mind and the soul, so that we can attain a lasting peace."

Buddha said, "Happiness comes when your work and words are of benefit to yourself and others." I derive happiness from thinking that perhaps I have contributed to you finding solace and comfort in your pursuit of peace for your soul.

I marvel at the calm found in a soul that stays *Still, in One Peace*. I find strength and encouragement when peace resides in the soul, and the healing, wholeness and fulfillment it provides to the broken pieces of life. I am a sojourner with you, on the journey to find peace. We share the same needs, dreams, desires and aspirations for lasting peace. I pray our shared journey has sustained you with the sustenance, hope and solitude I have found in writing this book.

The process of finding that place of peace, where we bring our mind to that still point of healing, often seems futile, like "trying to tame the wind."

We are not accustomed to being quiet and still. Our minds are preoccupied with issues and problems that cause us to be anxious and in despair. No matter what efforts we make to center our lives in tranquility, our brains struggle because they do not necessarily want to become still. Our soul becomes disquieted when we fail to infuse it with quietness and stillness, resulting in our unrest. Perhaps my words, along with other philosophical, inspirational or meditative disciplines, have engaged your mind and compelled your soul to be intentionally quiet and still, in your attempt to touch deeper places of solitude within your mind and soul.

Striving to find peace within my soul has a direct affect of providing peace of mind. I find that peace through God who dwells in my soul, every cell and every aspect of my being. I find it through my relationship with God who dwells within my mind and lives within my heart. As I strive to let God's mind live in my mind, I draw closer to the liberation from suffering, stress, turmoil, worry and unrest. The peaceful presence of God displaces those things from which I need liberation. God promises peace, a peace the world cannot give. Without God, the search for it will be a restless searching after things which can never satisfy my soul. Nor give my mind a chance to rest.

We cannot fully comprehend God's peace. It passes understanding! We must be engaged in its constant pursuit, until one day we clearly see the fullness of that peace. Since we cannot comprehend the depth of such peace, our mind is restless for the duration of our lives, as we strive to pacify it, stabilize it and create a peaceful equilibrium within it. We can *calm* the mind in pursuit of peace, as we take mental breaks, or find places to catch our second wind. Or as we do our breathing exercises. It is only within the soul, however, that we can bring our lives to that still place, that place of *rest*, where we reside completely in God's peace. The tranquility of the mind must be affected by the quietness of the soul. And the solitude in the soul must be in direct correlation to the serenity of our minds.

The Book of Psalms introduces one who struggles with the untamed mind and soul, as he tries to pacify it and grasp it. He asks, "Why are you cast down oh my soul?" A cast down soul is not at rest in the deep, lasting peace of God. "Hope thou in God!" the Psalmist claims, hope in the One who is our only true peace. The pursuit of peace is a lifelong engagement. We recognize the length of that journey in the church's liturgy for the burial of the dead, when at the end of our physical journey we find the fullness of peace in the life that finally rests in the peace of God and in the comfort of God's Spirit. The liturgy asks that God grant, to the one who has died, the peace for which that life has searched its whole lifespan on earth. "Grant them peace, eternal rest" "Perpetual light." The fullness of the lasting peace found in the promise of Eternal Life, where we will be forever *Still, in One Peace.*

In Psalm 104 we read of God's creative genius and design in creating peace out of turmoil and chaos. When tempest waves and storms rage violently across the seas, God's touch calms those waves and establishes peace on earth. God's touch brings order, stillness, peace and harmony to all of nature. From God's chamber in heaven God casts the beams of light upon the tempest waves and at God's rebuke the waves become calm. Our lives are formed and shaped by that same touch. The world sings in harmony and offers its praise. From our hearts that are *Still, in One Peace*, at peace in the Creator's love, we offer the same praise:

You bound the world together so that it would never fall apart. You clothed the earth with floods of waters covering up the mountains. You spoke, and at the sound of your shout the water collected into its vast ocean beds, and mountains rose and valleys sank to the levels you decreed. And then you set a boundary for the seas, so that they would never again cover the earth. God placed springs in the valleys and streams that gush from the mountains. They give water for all the animals to drink. There the wild donkeys quench their thirst, and the birds nest beside the steams and sing among the branches of the trees. He sends rain upon the mountains and fills the earth with fruit. The tender grass grows up at his command to feed the cattle, and there are fruit trees, vegetables and grain for man to cultivate, and wine to make him glad, and olive oil as lotion for his skin, and bread to give him strength. There before me lies the mighty ocean, teeming with life of every kind, both great and small. And look! See the ships! And over there, the whale you made to play in the sea. Every one of these depends on you to give them daily food. You supply it, and they gather it. You open wide your hand to feed them and they are satisfied with all your bountiful provision. Then you send your Spirit, and new life is born to replenish all the living of the earth. Praise God forever! How he must rejoice in all his work! I will sing to the Lord as long as I live. I will praise God to my last breath! May God be pleased by all these thoughts about him, for he is the source of all my joy.

This portrait of the Creator, a God who designs order, purpose and promise, reveals a God who binds the world together so that it would never fall apart. He holds us in His love so that we will never fall apart. If we do fall apart, winding up in pieces, He does not leave us splintered. No storm, nothing, can shake our innermost calm.

God's provisions are boundless. God's grace, abundant. He sustains us. When the journey is rough, He gently supports us. If we make a mess, if we lose our way, grace tenderly leads us home. Love reshapes our brokenness. His peace restores the form of love we lost.

I trust God to be the source of my peace. In Him, my life is *Still, in One Peace*. Being still in this assurance, that pacifies my mind. The peace I find within my soul is a peace that flows into all the areas of my being – mind, body and spirit. My life wants to sing of the goodness, grace and peace that God provides.

It is the nature of the mind not to become still. Try getting a child to sit still in a chair, on the floor, in the car, at church, for more than a few moments; especially without a CP or Gameboy. You will discover the true nature of the mind. It rebels. People check their watches during an hour of worship. They are restless, even while in the place with the One to whom they have turned to find the stillness that can bring peace to their hearts throughout the week. Restlessness is a mindset of children as well as adults. We simply don't want to be still, in our quick-fix world.

It's hard to give the mind a break from preoccupation with concerns, issues, agendas, worries or fears. Getting a hold of the mind is an unending discipline. Otherwise the mind stays turbulent. It will never be at rest. Never rest in the One who holds our lives in the deep peace of His love and goodness.

God replenishes our lives. This assurance of God's goodness causes me to want to sing to Him as long as I live. With praises to God to my last breath! The birds rest in the nests besides the streams and sing in the branches of the trees. May he be pleased, as well, by all these thoughts about Him, for He is the source of all my joy. He is the source of my inner peace. He is the place in which I bring my life to be *Still, in One Peace.* I can't keep my voice from singing!

The desire to still the mind is a universal practice. It has nothing to do with religion. Gandhi said, "God has no religion." I have been influenced by the wisdom of the ages and the sages, insights of world religions, as well as the truth I find in my faith that forms my understanding of God, life, others and myself. I ask this question many times: "Would I rather have the world in the palm of my hands or have a world of peace in the center of my soul and heart?"

On Fifth Avenue in Manhattan, there is the famed statue of Atlas, bending on his knees with the weight of the world saddled on his muscular shoulders. Across the street from Atlas, is St. Patrick's Cathedral. In one of the chapels that adorn the nave there is a statue of Jesus as a boy. In His hand he holds the world. While Atlas buckles beneath the load of the world upon his back, a young Christ child has the world in His hand. In His control. This reassures me, as I find my life held in the palm of God's hand, from who I receive everything I need, all the provisions to refresh my spirit, all the grace to sustain my life. All the promises to hold me still, in His One peace as I journey through this life. The Old Testament says, "In His hand, are the souls of the righteous and there no torment shall harm them." This is cause for endless singing! I find true peace, and I can truly sing, when I am held in Christ's hand.

Robert Wadsworth Lowry wrote a hymn that reflects the peace within my life and the reason I can't contain my praise and song, or keep from writing about the promise of God's peace. In Lowry's lyric I find the assurance and strength of peace that is promised in all circumstances, especially in those that threaten to keep any one of us in broken pieces.

Considering all we encounter in life, we can have a faith and trust in God who brings us to rest, to be *Still, In One Peace*, moving us beyond merely surviving in one piece. We can have a trusting faith that rests in God's assurances and find ourselves still, at rest, in that One peace:

My life flows on in endless song
above earth's lamentation,
I catch the sweet, tho far off hymn
that hails a new creation
through all the tumult and the strife
I hear the music ringing,
It finds an echo in my soul
How can I keep from singing?
What tho my joy and comfort die?
The Lord my Savior liveth,
What tho the darkness gather round?
songs in the night He giveth
No storm can shake my inmost calm,
while to that refuge clinging;
since Christ is Lord of heaven and earth
How can I keep from singing?
I lift my eyes, the clouds grow thin
I see the blue above it;
And day by day the pathway smoothes,
Since first I learned to love it.
The peace of Christ makes fresh my heart
A fountain ever springing
All things are mine since I am His
How can I keep from singing?

This song summarizes all that has been written in this book, conveying the hope we can find by centering our lives *Still, in One Peace.* The wisdom from the sages, and my attempts to reflect their insights for our living, and the solitude, peacefulness and hope that comes from residing our hearts and minds in God, through all these we can find that peace that gives our lives an endless song.

Still your mind. Center down in that One who brings stillness to our souls. Peace within. Let our minds, being in repose, become the mirror of the universe, the speculum of all creation. The fullness of God's love.

Through this book I have lifted my voice, daring to lift my words and place them as drops into the pools of wisdom throughout the ages, hoping that through them we can continue to desire God intensely, yet in stillness. Quietly, with all our heart, mind and strength.

As we do, we will find our lives *Still, in One Peace.*

The only "ism" necessary is not any form of religion. What only is needed is the God who keeps us *Still, in His One Peace.* Find yourself in the only "ism" that will provide a lasting peace. ISM. In Silent Meditation.

Be still in the meditations of your heart.

Listen!

Can you hear the echo in your soul? Can you hear the voice of God ringing? Be still, and know that One peace.

How can you keep from singing? Especially when the fullness of God's love within you brings you to that place where you will always be

Still, in One peace!

(Listen to the recording of *How Can I Keep from Singing*, from Shepherd Moons, by Enya as inspiration for reading this closing chapter of *Still, In One Peace*)

Circle Books

Circle is a symbol of infinity and unity. It's part of a growing list of imprints, including o-books.net and zero-books.net.

Circle Books aims to publish books in Christian spirituality that are fresh, accessible, and stimulating.

Our books are available in all good English language bookstores worldwide. If you can't find the book on the shelves, then ask your bookstore to order it for you, quoting the ISBN and title. Or, you can order online—all major online retail sites carry our titles.

To see our list of titles, please view www.Circle-Books.com, growing by 80 titles per year.

Authors can learn more about our proposal process by going to our website and clicking on Your Company > Submissions.

We define Christian spirituality as the relationship between the self and its sense of the transcendent or sacred, which issues in literary and artistic expression, community, social activism, and practices. A wide range of disciplines within the field of religious studies can be called upon, including history, narrative studies, philosophy, theology, sociology, and psychology. Interfaith in approach, Circle Books fosters creative dialogue with non-Christian traditions.

And tune into MySpiritRadio.com for our book review radio show, hosted by June-Elleni Laine, where you can listen to authors discussing their books.

MySpiritRadio